Bushido

A Complete History of British Jujutsu

Simon Keegan

NEW HAVEN PUBLISHING LTD

First Edition Published 2019
NEW HAVEN PUBLISHING LTD

www.newhavenpublishingltd.com
newhavenpublishing@gmail.com

newhaven
publishing

Contents

Introduction

Jujutsu has been in Britain for longer than Karate has been in Japan. British Jujutsu pre-dates Aikido. It pre-dates Shotokan, Goju Ryu and Wado Ryu. When Jujutsu was introduced to the UK, Judo was only 10 years old. It pre-dates the Dai Nippon Butokukai and has been a part of the English language since the days of Rudyard Kipling.

When Jujutsu was introduced to Britain it was the era of 'Jack the Ripper' and 'Sherlock Holmes' (Holmes even studied Jujutsu, or, as it was called, *Baritsu*). Yet there has never been a comprehensive history of British Jujutsu written. Having written a book on the history of Okinawan martial arts, called *Karate Jutsu*, I had no immediate plans to write such a work on Jujutsu. But I was inspired to do so upon meeting Sensei David Brough. He and I shared notes and collaborated, and this book would not be possible without his considerable input.

Who were the pioneers of British Jujutsu? Some go without saying, men like EW Barton Wright (of *Bartitsu* fame, the inspiration for Holmes' *Baritsu*) pictured below, who promoted the art in Victorian and Edwardian music halls.

But others have been almost forgotten, men like Liverpool's Harry Hunter and Gerry Skyner.

There's a saying, 'history is written by the winners,' and in some respects that's true of British Jujutsu. Those with successful students are upheld in folk memory for longer. What I have tried to do is consult contemporary records where possible. For example, in the 1930s there are numerous records in the local newspapers of Skyner teaching Jujutsu but none I can find of Jack Britten, but perhaps because Britten's students went on to establish governing bodies it is he who is remembered as the city's pioneer.

Throughout the research for this book I came across many Jujutsu pioneers with what are clearly fictional back stories. Normally we find that they alone were trained by some mysterious master of a style that was passed only to them. In the valley of the blind (otherwise known as the pre Internet age) the one eyed man was clearly king. I have not laboured my own views as to the existence of their seemingly fictional lineages but have instead offered actual evidence through contemporary records and photographs through which I believe the reader can be the judge.

There have been many important influences on the early development of British Jujutsu.

One is the publication of an earlier book called *The Text Book of Ju Jutsu as Practised in Japan* written by Raku Uyenishi in 1905. My father gave me two antique volumes of this book, and it is clear that it is a template for much of what we know today as British Jujutsu. My father began his own Jujutsu studies in a style which, I would discover, was influenced by this work.

Uyenishi's students were also prolific authors of Jujutsu and formed the British Ju Jitsu Society (BJJS).

While Tani and Koizumi migrated to Judo, the BJJS continued to practise Jujutsu as taught by Uyenishi.

Of course many subsequent developments by Britten, Skyner, James Blundell, Robert Clark, Kenshiro Abbe, Vernon Bell and many others shaped British Jujutsu as we know it today.

When Tani and Uyenishi arrived in the UK the Jujutsu they taught was adapted to deal with British fighting styles such as wrestling and boxing, rapidly establishing a British Jujutsu style, which is unique from the Koryu parent styles.

Sadakuza (Raku) Uyenishi was in the UK for only seven years, yet we find his legacy is significant within British Jujutsu today. It was Barton-Wright who took Uyenishi to London in 1900, but from the available evidence it would seem that it was the Jujutsu of Uyenishi that provided the greatest influence on the development of British Jujutsu.

While this book is comprehensive in covering the major events and pioneers of the art, the omission of styles and teachers, many no doubt important and influential, is not a reflection on how I view their importance and nor does it diminish their contribution. I can't list every one of thousands of Jujutsu instructors, so I have tried to just cover the pioneers and major school founders.

My own story goes back further than some might think. My great uncle Bill Nelson was a black belt in Gerry Skyner's early club in the 1940s and then moved over to Gunji Koizumi's Arnot Street School, and Koizumi's relationship with Liverpool dates back to 1906.

Bill therefore trained in two of Liverpool's earliest Jujutsu schools. Bill and his older brother, my grandad Jim, had previously been taught boxing and unarmed combat by their father Willy 'Elmo' Nelson and their Swedish grandfather August Nilsson. August, like his father Nils Johann before him, learnt combatives in the Swedish Royal Navy. Willy served with the King's Regiment in World War I. Jim was also in the army in World War II and Billy was in the merchant navy. Jim's brother-in-law Ted Molloy (cousin of Liverpool boxing champions Tommy and Jimmy Molloy) was a master-at-arms in the Royal Navy who served in Japan and China. Therefore when my great uncle began training with Gerry Skyner, Jujutsu was not entirely new to him. His father taught boxing and unarmed combat to all the lads in the street, and the combatives he learnt in the war were Jujutsu based.

My father David Keegan and his twin brother Paul commenced Jujutsu training in around 1959 with the Blundells in Kirkby. Like my great uncle Billy, Jim Blundell had been in the merchant navy in the war.

So my own journey started at home. My father, uncles, grandfather and great uncles all encouraged me on the martial path. Over the years I trained with many instructors in Jujutsu, Karate, Kung Fu, Aikido, Judo, Iaido and more.

At the age of 16 I began the next stage of my journey, studying under Steve Bullough of the Bushido Academy, who was my mentor for 8 years and changed my life in ways I only understood many years later.

I came to study with many other teachers and become a member of Japan's oldest Budo fraternities, such as the Kokusai Budoin and Dai Nippon Butokukai. I was lucky to get on the mat with some of the last of a generation of Japanese Jujutsu masters and also to train with some of the pioneers of British Karate and Jujutsu.

I have tried to write this history in a way that Jujutsu practitioners – and other martial arts exponents – can enjoy it, learn from it and understand their own art's roots. It is written with no political bias towards associations and I believe I have been fair to all.

Simon Keegan *Kyoshi*, 6th Dan

Acknowledgements

I would like to particularly thank David Brough, Historian of the Bushido Ju Jitsu Academy and the British Ju Jitsu Association (GB), and members of the BJJA(GB) for their contributions to this book.

They are:

James Pape (10th dan)
Robert Ashworth (8th dan)
Richard Asbery (7th dan)
Dave Bushell (5th dan)
David Brough (3rd dan)
Andy Smith (3rd dan)

Paul Geoghegan (9th dan)
John Idle (7th dan)
Philip Rhodes (6th dan)
Andy Walker (5th dan)
Chris Henry (3rd dan)
Gavin Davies (2nd dan)

I would also like to especially thank for their generous contributions:

Paul Masters (Menkyo Kaiden), Tenjin Shinyo Ryu
Lee Masters (Menkyo Kaiden), Tenjin Shinyo Ryu
Andy Howarth (7th Dan), Grassendale Ju Jitsu Do

Thanks to:

James McDade (10th dan), Total Self Defence
Alfie Lewis (9th dan), World Martial arts Organisation
Martin Dixon (9th dan), Masters of Martial Arts, BJJAGB (Chairman)
Kenny Blundell (9th dan), The Lowlands Ju Jitsu Association, BJJAGB
Terry Wingrove (9th dan), Seibukan, International Ju Jitsu Federation
Mark Wood (8th dan), United Kingdom Budo Federation
Eric Marshall (8th dan), BKR Ju Jitsu
Stephen McDade (8th dan), Total Self Defence
Robert Hart (7th dan), The World Ju Jitsu Federation (WJJF)
Ian Arbon (7th dan), Wakarashin Jujitsu, BJJAGB
Mark Fitzgerald (7th dan), Kokora Kai Jujitsu, BJJAGB
Julian Mallalieu (6th dan), United Kingdom Budo Federation
Travis Boggs (5th dan), Ju-Jutsu Historical Research Society, U.S.A.
David Howard (4th dan), The World Ju Jitsu Federation (WJJF)
Lee Hallard (4th dan, Jujutsu/Aikido), Aiki Shin Liverpool
Wayne Blundell (3rd dan), The Lowlands Ju Jitsu Association, BJJAGB
Dave Williams (3rd dan), Budokan Ju Jitsu Club
Scott Mallon (3rd dan), Stanford Warriors Ju Jitsu Association
Kirby Watson (Menkyo), Kaze Arashi Ryu
Jimmy Davison, The Alpha Ju Jitsu Institute
Beryl Miao, The World Ju Jitsu Federation (WJJF)
Mike Callan (7th dan Judo), University of Hertfordshire

Tony Underwood (6th dan Judo), BJC
Brian N Watson (4th dan Judo), Judo Author/Historian
Ross Taylor (2nd dan Judo), British Judo
Michael Manning, senior student of Vernon Bell
Tony Wolf, the Bartitsu Society
Joseph Svinth, EJMAS
Lizzie Richmond, University of Bath (the Bowen Collection)
Andrew Colwell (son of Ronnie Colwell)
Lorraine Wells (great-granddaughter of W Bruce Sutherland)

I would like to dedicate this book to all my teachers past and present including:

David Keegan (5th dan)
My father and lifelong guide, 40 years and counting

Steve Bullough (8th dan)
My early Sensei in Bushido for 8 years

The late Phil Handyside (9th dan)
My mentor and friend in Karate for 17 years

The late Allan Tattersall (9th dan)
A friend and teacher in Jujutsu and Iaido

Many others who helped me on the path including: Bob Carruthers 8th dan, Jack Hearn 9th dan, Terry Wingrove 9th dan, the late Shizuya Sato 10th dan, Reiner Parsons 8th dan and his teacher Tadanori Nobetsu 10th dan, Fumio Demura 9th dan, Patrick McCarthy 9th dan, Ray Walker 3rd dan, the late Steve Brennan 3rd dan, the late Alan Ruddock 6th dan.

Jujutsu, Ju-Jitsu or Jiu Jitsu

Firstly, I will begin with the definition. You will see several variations of the name: Jujitsu, Jiu jitsu, and Jujutsu. Which one is correct?

The standard way to Romanise Japanese is to use Hepburn Romanisation. 柔 is Ju, or rather Juu (this character is also pronounced Yawara), meaning soft. The u in Ju is actually a long vowel (u+u) and so would be pronounced Juu or the long u would be denoted with a macron e.g. Jū. Japanese will pronounce Jū as 'Joo'. There is no syllable in Japanese that should be pronounced Ji-yoo and so Jiu is incorrect.

The second character of the kanji, 術, means art or technique. Here the u is short. A Japanese person would also pronounce the letter 'i' differently (e.g. 'ee'), and thus if a Japanese person were to see the word Jitsu they would pronounce it 'Jeets'. So the correct or standard Hepburn Romanisation is Jujutsu or Jūjutsu. This detail was not lost on the first Japanese to bring Jujutsu to the UK. For example Sadakazu Uyenishi, then based in London, titled his 1905 book *The Text Book of Ju-Jutsu as Practised in Japan*.

In his book from 1923 *Ju-Jutsu & Judo* Percy Longhurst states on his first page *'It is no more than thirty years ago since Ju-Jutsu (less correctly Ju-Jitsu) found its way into England.'* However, from early on the term Ju Jitsu became widely used in the UK. To keep things simple in this book I will refer to the martial art as Jujutsu except where 'Jiu' or 'Jitsu' have been used in the title of a style, organisation, or club.

It is also possible to define Japanese martial arts as either Koryu or Gendai, which mean 'old tradition' or 'modern' respectively. Unlike the martial traditions of some countries, in Japan there is a clear definition and that is the Meiji Restoration of 1868. The Meiji Restoration marks the time when power was removed from the Shogun - thereby ending the rule of the Samurai class - and returned to the Emperor. Therefore at this point the martial arts stopped being monopolised by professional warriors and were available to most social classes. In Japan the professional warrior clans appointed ryuha (hereditary tradition) to pass on their warrior traditions.

Within most ryu (style, or school) the senior member of the clan would inherit the title of Soke or Iemoto. This in a sense was equivalent to grandmaster, but was by birthright rather than skill, so a better translation would simply be 'inheritor'. For example in Tenshin Shoden Katori Shinto Ryu the title of Soke was inherited for some 600 years within the Iizasa family until one died without an heir. The school was kept running until a male married into the family. The current Soke Iizasa Shuri-no-Suke Yasusada is not regarded as a martial artist *par excellence* and instead the school is run by a Shihan (head-teacher) named Risuke Otake. Therefore Katori has in effect two lineages; the Soke line by blood, and the Shihan line by teaching. The Katori syllabus includes Kenjutsu (sword),

Naginatajutsu (halberd), Bojutsu (staff), Sojutsu (spear), Jujutsu (lightly armed grappling), and Shurikenjutsu (dart throwing). Each of these styles has a set number of kata (set routines) and the number of formal kata in the ryu may amount to around 100. To be an official student of Katori, you need to take a blood oath before Otake Sensei and only he can authorise your certificates of proficiency. This is another hallmark of the Koryu.

In Koryu, rather than coloured belts (kyu) and black belt (dan) grades, students are awarded certificates of competence. So one might receive a 'Menkyo Oku Iri' in Jujutsu, a 'Menkyo Mokuroku' in Kenjutsu, and finally, when you have passed the entire curriculum, you may be awarded a 'Menkyo Kaiden' which means 'licence of total transmission'. In Koryu it is common to receive a Menkyo Kaiden while relatively young; therefore it cannot be compared to the proverbial 10th dan. In Koryu a closer equivalent would be a provisional, full, and advanced driver's licence.

In some ryu the styles taught can be varied. There is almost always a primary weapon like the katana (sword), but the ryu may also teach swimming, horsemanship or espionage. Koryu differs from Gendai in what is authentically recognised.

For example, if we take Aikido as an example of Gendai Budo, it is not necessary to be recognised by the Ueshiba family to teach. There are many styles, like Yoseikan, Yoshinkan and Shudokan and Gendai Budo (martial arts), which can be combined to form new Budo. For example Yoseikan is a blend of Aikido, Judo, Karate, Kobudo and other styles. For the most part, as we will see below, British Jujutsu, and Brazilian Jujutsu, can be considered Gendai Budo forms. Furthermore, in Gendai Budo, ranks can be cross awarded. For example the Goju Ryu master Morio Higaonna was awarded one of his senior grades by a Shorin Ryu instructor. In Koryu one would seldom if ever find a Muso Shinden Ryu teacher endorsing grades in Yagyu Shingan Ryu.

If an instructor claims to be a senior teacher of a Koryu, they should be in possession of formal certification (Menkyo) and should be registered in Japan. Of course there are many instructors who have trained in Koryu but only teach what they have learnt as part of a wider syllabus.

When Jujutsu was first introduced to Britain, the likes of Gunji Koizumi and Yukio Tani had almost certainly trained in Koryu but were not representative head-teachers of a ryu. It is unlikely that any British teachers prior to the 1950s were certified by a Koryu.

As we will see below, there are British instructors who have studied Koryu - Quintin Chambers for example was exposed to Katori, Mike Finn studied Shindo Muso Ryu, Allan Tattersall trained in Takenouchi Ryu, and Paul Masters became a Menkyo Kaiden in Tenjin Shinyo Ryu.

Furthermore hundreds of British Iaidoka have studied Muso Jikiden Eishin Ryu and Muso Shinden Ryu. But the early pioneers of British Jujutsu taught systems very unique to these isles.

The Koryu Styles

There are a number of Koryu that are important for the development of British Jujutsu. I will discuss some of these here, delving in to detail where it has been possible and is relevant. The first Koryu I consider is Daito Ryu.

Takeda Sokaku, 35th generation restorer of Daito Ryu

Daito Ryu

In order to understand Daito Ryu Jujutsu we need to start with the 35th generation Soke Takeda Sokaku, because this is when the style began to forge its identity.

Takeda Sokaku was born in 1859 in the Aizu domain (Fukushima) around the time of the Boshin War. His father Takeda Sokichi was a low level Samurai who worked as a farmer, albeit one with a proud heritage, and he was a Sumo champion. Sokaku's maternal grandfather was Dengoro Kurokochi, a Yari and

Kenjutsu master. The young Sokaku studied spear with the Hozoin Ryu Takada-ha and sword with the Ono-ha Itto Ryu and Kashima Shinden Jikishinkage Ryu. Sokaku was also a direct descendant of the legendary general Takeda Shingen and combined two lines of Takeda family traditions to formalise the Daito Ryu that we know today.

Daito Ryu is one of the most famous Ryuha because of its strong influence on Aikido, Hakko Ryu and Hapkido.

When Sokaku passed succession to his son Tokimume it appeared as if the succession of an ancient ryu had been passed on. However, Takeda was actually considered the 'restorer' of Daito Ryu, and had pieced together the school from different sources. Because Sokaku was the heir to the Takeda family traditions it was his prerogative to do this, but it is for this reason that Daito Ryu may not always be considered Koryu as Sokaku formally established the school after the Meiji Restoration. However, since Takeda restored Daito Ryu by piecing together aspects of his own clan traditions, based on his studies with his pre-Meiji Restoration father and grandfather, it is my opinion that Daito Ryu is indeed Koryu.

As the Meiji Restoration came into effect, Sokaku began to prioritise Jujutsu more than ancient weaponry and became a student of Saigo Shiro (Hoshina Chikanori), whose 'oshikiuchi' system was the official system of Aizu retainers. It is important to reiterate that the oshikiuchi system also came from the Takeda clan. It may not be a coincidence that Takeda lent his support to Saigo Tanomo's namesake Saigo Takamori, who was leading a Samurai rebellion against the Meiji government (as depicted in the movie *The Last Samurai*).

At some point Sokaku began to refer to his school as Daito Ryu Aikijujutsu, but according to his son, Aiki was a term used in the Edo period. Of the term Aikijujutsu, Takeda Tokimune said: *'I think that aiki was taught as a self-defence art beginning a long time ago, during the Tokugawa period. Among the Daito Ryu jujutsu techniques is a particular type of aiki technique that we call hanza handachi. Techniques that were studied for use in the palace are called oshikiuchi. In the old days when people passed into the obanbeya of Edo castle, all of their swords were taken away. Everyone - except for those nobles of a certain rank, who were allowed to keep their short swords - had to surrender all of their weapons. They had to walk on their knees in front of the family of the Shogun. The hanza handachi techniques of the Daito Ryu were used during that period in response to any situation that might arise.'*

Among Sokaku's most notable students were Yoshida Kotaro (awarded Kyoju Dairi), Morihei Ueshiba (founder of Aikido), Tokuma Hisa (awarded Menkyo Kaiden), Yukiyoshi Sagawa (awarded Kyoju Dairi), and Yamamoto Kakuyoshi (awarded Kyoju Dairi).

The origins of Daito Ryu trace back to one of the legendary Japanese emperors, via Shinra Saburo Minamoto no Yoshimitsu (1045–1127), who was a Minamoto clan Samurai and member of the Seiwa Genji. Daito Ryu is said to take its name from the mansion that Yoshimitsu lived in as a child. Takeda Tokimune described the origins as follows: *'It can be said that Emperor Seiwa is the founder of Daito Ryu. When the youngest grandson of Emperor Seiwa, Shinra Saburo Yoshimitsu, went to Oshu in the northeastern district of Japan, he studied human anatomy through dissection, and this was the origin of Daito Ryu. He stayed at a place known as Daito, and called himself Saburo of Daito. This is the source of the name. Daito Ryu was then passed down through generations of the Takeda family, as we are also descendants of the Emperor Seiwa.'*

Daito Ryu lineage:

1 Emperor Seiwa
2 Prince Sadazumi
3 Minamoto no Tsunemoto
4 Minamoto no Mitsunaka
5 Minamoto no Yorinobu
6 Minamoto no Yoriyoshi
7 Minamoto Yoshimitsu –

Yoshimitsu moved to Kai Province (Yamanashi Prefecture), and passed on his martial arts within his family. Yoshimitsu's great-grandson Nobuyoshi adopted the surname 'Takeda', which has been the name of the family to the present day.

8 Minamoto Yoshikiyo
9 Minamoto Kiyomitsu
10 Takeda Nobuyoshi
11 Takeda Nobumitsu
12 Takeda Nobumasa
Six missing generations

19 Takeda Nobumitsu

Four missing generations

24 Takeda Nobutora
25 Takeda Shingen
26 Takeda Katsuyori

Takeda Shingen opposed Tokugawa Ieyasu and Oda Nobunaga in their campaign to unify and control all of Japan. With the death of Shingen and his heir, Takeda Katsuyori, the Takeda family relocated to the Aizu domain. Takeda Shingen was the first-born son of Takeda Nobutora, leader of the Takeda clan, and daimyo of the province of Kai. In 1536, at the age of 15, Shingen was instrumental in helping his father win the Battle of Un no Kuchi. At some point in his life after his 'coming of age' ceremony Shingen decided to rebel against Nobutora. He finally succeeded in 1540, taking control of the clan. It is thought that Nobutora had planned to name the second son, Nobushige, as his heir instead of Shingen. After Shingen's death Takeda Katsuyori became the daimyo of the Takeda clan. Katsuyori was ambitious and desired to continue the legacy of his father. He moved on to take Tokugawa forts. However, an allied force of Tokugawa Ieyasu and Oda Nobunaga dealt a crushing blow to the Takeda in the Battle of Nagashino. Katsuyori committed suicide after the battle, and the Takeda clan never recovered. Here we see two lineages emerging, the continuing Takeda line and the Hoshina line.

27 Takeda Chikara (Daito Ryu)	Hoshina Masayuki (Oshikiuchi)
28 Takeda Nobutsugu (Daito Ryu)	Hoshina Masatune (Oshikiuchi)
29 Unknown Takeda(Daito Ryu)	Matsudaira Masayoshi (Oshikiuchi)
30 Unknown Takeda (Daito Ryu)	Matsudaira Yoshizumi (Oshikiuchi)
31 Unknown Takeda (Daito Ryu)	Matsudaira Yoshichika (Oshikiuchi)
32 Unknown Takeda (Daito Ryu)	Matsudaira Yoshitaka (Oshikiuchi)

Tokugawa Ieyasu's grandson, Komatsumaru (1611–1673), was adopted by Takeda Kenshoin (fourth daughter of Takeda Shingen). Komatsumaru devoted himself to the study of the Takeda family's martial arts, and was subsequently adopted by Hoshina Masamitsu. Komatsumaru changed his name to Hoshina Masayuki and in 1644 was appointed the governor of Aizu.

As governor, he mandated that all subsequent rulers of Aizu study the arts of Ono-ha Itto Ryu (which he himself had mastered), as well as the art of Oshikiuchi, a martial art which he developed for shogunate counsellors and retainers, tailored to conditions within the palace. These arts became incorporated into and combined with the Takeda family martial arts and were passed on together.

33 Takeda Soemon (Daito Ryu)	Matsudaira Yoshiyasu (Oshikiuchi)
34 Takeda Sokichi (Daito Ryu)	Saigo Tanomo (Oshikiuchi)
35 Takeda Sokaku (Restorer of Daito Ryu)	

Students of Takeda Sokaku included:
- Yoshida Kotaro (awarded Kyoju Dairi)
- Morihei Ueshiba (founder of Aikido)
- Tokuma Hisa (awarded Menkyo Kaiden)
- Yukiyoshi Sagawa (awarded Kyoju Dairi)
- Yamamoto Kakuyoshi (awarded Kyoju Dairi)
- Minoru Mochizuki (received Hiden Mokuroku)

36 Takeda Tokimune

Students of Takeda Tokimune included:
- Katsuyuki Kondo
- Shigemitsu Kato
- Gunpachi Arisawa

Yoshida Kotaro was a master of Daito Ryu Aikijujutsu (he held the title of Kyoju Dairi from the grandmaster of the style, Takeda Sokaku, and at one point was considered his successor) and he was also the head of his family's style, Yanagi Ryu, which is thought to be derived from Yoshin Ryu, a method of Hakuda. He is significant to British Jujutsu because he is believed to have taught Kawaishi Mikonosuke, who taught in London and Liverpool.

Of Morihei Ueshiba training with his father, Tokimune said: '*Mr. Ueshiba studied Daito-Ryu with my father from 1915 through 1919, about five years. He trained extensively and was enthusiastic. He was Sokaku's favourite student. However, I was the one who was scolded most frequently by Sokaku. After me, it was Morihei Ueshiba whom he scolded most often. Since I was Sokaku's son I wasn't so bothered when he scolded me, but I imagine that Mr. Ueshiba must have been greatly affected since he wasn't a member of the family....Mr. Ueshiba also accompanied Sokaku a great deal. Traveling with Sokaku was more significant than just studying with him during the regular practice sessions. And what's more, Mr. Ueshiba also taught as Sokaku's assistant....He was very devoted to Daito-Ryu and also quite talkative. When Sokaku was teaching a group of judges and public prosecutors in Hakodate, Mr. Ueshiba happened to be his companion and assisted in teaching them....Morihei Ueshiba was a splendid person even at such a young age.*' Ueshiba's students include his son Kisshomaru, Minoru Mochizuki (Yoseikan), Kenji Tomiki (Shudokan), Takuma Hisa (also a student of Takeda), Gozo Shioda (Yoshinkan), Koichi Tohei (Ki Aikido), Kenshiro Abbe, and Alan Ruddock, a pioneer of the art in Ireland.

Eishin Ryu

Although not thought of as a Jujutsu school, the Eishin Ryu contained empty handed techniques and influenced the formation of many British Jujutsu schools - as well as Iaido and Kendo clubs. Muso Jikiden Eishin Ryu (peerless, directly transmitted school of Eishin) was derived from the old school of Hasegawa Eishin Ryu, in turn coming from Shinmei Muso Ryu. The style was named after Hasegawa Chikaranosuke Eishin as a continuation of the teachings he received in Shinmei Muso Ryu. The 9th generation Soke was Hayashi Rokudayu Morimasa. Hayashi introduced a set of techniques (part of the Omori Ryu sub style) executed from a kneeling position. These techniques are thought to have been developed by Hayashi's Kenjutsu teacher, the Shinkage Ryu swordsman Omori Rokurozaemon. These kneeling forms are now fairly synonymous with Iaido. They are influenced by Ogasawara Ryu, which saw Bushi kneeling in certain social situations. There were also elaborate leg movements to allow for a long hakama.

The Katana developed as warfare evolved in Japan. Originally the Tachi (longsword) was worn slung from the belt, blade down like a cavalry sabre, cutlass or scimitar. As Bushi began to spend less time riding into battle and more time having to defend themselves around the towns and cities, the cavalry weapon gave way to the Daisho (big and small), a Katana and Wakizashi twin swords worn thrust through the belt with the blades up to allow for a standing cut. As the art of Kenjutsu or Tojutsu ('Ken' and 'To' are variations of the Chinese 'Jian' and 'Dao') developed, two distinct practice methods evolved: one was the ability to draw the sword and execute fast cuts with surgical precision; the other was the ability to fence with an opponent. The former evolved into Iaido, the latter into Kendo. Generally Bushi did not take their swords indoors with them, so at dinners when kneeling they might be more likely to defend with short swords or knives which were left in the belt.

After the death of the 11th head-master, Oguro Motoemon Kiyokatsu, the school split into two factions or 'ha'. One branch, the Shimomura-ha, was renamed by its fourteenth head-master Hosokawa Yoshimasa to Muso Shinden Eishin Ryu. After studying under Hosokawa, Nakayama Hakudo created his own branch in 1932, commonly called Muso Shinden Ryu. Because of his position in the martial arts organisation Kokusai Budoin (see below), Nakayama taught a number of notable martial artists. He taught for many years at a Japanese military academy, and from his teachings there arose a new method called Toyama Ryu Batto Jutsu, a very simple efficient style of Iai with the 20th century soldier in mind. In 1939, a 27-year-old Kendo instructor by the name of Nakamura Taizburo was selected to attend the Academy. After six months Taizburo qualified to be an instructor of Jissen Budo, the combat martial arts of sword, knife and bayonet. This marked a major turning point in the evolution of Toyama Ryu Batto Jutsu.

While teaching Kenjutsu in China, Nakamura Taizburo, who also studied calligraphy, was inspired with the thought that eiji happo, the eight rules of calligraphy, might also apply to swordsmanship. While practising the ei character, he saw that the eight brush strokes traced the trajectory of the sword while cutting. From this came the realisation that there were only eight distinct cuts possible with the sword; all others were just variations of the theme. One of the most notable instructors of Toyama Ryu in the world is Karate and Kobudo master Fumio Demura.

My father David Keegan performing Muso Jikiden Eishin Ryu at a Japanese cultural festival. The Taiko drums can be seen behind him.

The other branch, the Tanimura-ha, was renamed Muso Jikiden Eishin Ryu during the Taisho era (1912-1926) by its 17th head-master, Oe Masamichi, who incorporated the Shimomura-ha techniques and standardised the curriculum. Today there are a number of branches, including some taught in the UK.

Ichitaro Kuroda was a notable instructor of Muso Shinden Ryu, a style somewhat introduced to the UK by his student Mike Finn. In addition to his 9th dan in Kendo and mastership of Muso Shinden Ryu, Kuroda was also a master of Shindo Muso Ryu, a Koryu best known for its use of the Jo staff.

Muso Jikiden Eishin Ryu is taught by the Kokusai Budoin (International Martial Arts Federation) and its head-masters have included Tsugiyoshi Ota (Meijin Iaido 10th dan), Katsuo Yamaguchi (Meijin Iaido 10th dan), Tadao Ochiai (Hanshi Iaido 10th dan), and Keiji Tose, (Hanshi Iaido 10th dan).

Another Eishin Ryu master who came to the UK was Fuji Okimitsu, who taught the likes of Allan Tattersall and Steve Rowe. Fuji Okimitsu was born in 1939 in Saga Prefecture, which is the old province of Hizen, and lived in Dartford, Kent for many years and later Cornwall. He was a key figure in the development of the British Kendo Association (he held membership no. 1). Fuji was also associated with the legendary Haruna Matsuo, All Japan Iaido champion.

| 居合道 Iaido | 無双直伝英信流 Musojikiden Eishin ryu | (創始 林崎甚助源重信) | I.MA.F. | No 1 |

正座の部 Seizanobu			立膝の部 Tachihizanobu			抜刀流 Battoho		
番号 No.	名称 name	ローマ字 roman letter	番号 No.	名称 name	ローマ字 roman letter	番号 No.	名称 name	ローマ字 roman letter
1	前	Mae	1	横雲	Yokogumo		1	順刀 No.1	Junto No.1
2	右	Migi	2	虎一足	Toraisshoku	基	2	順刀 No.2	Junto No.2
3	左	Hidari	3	稲妻	Inazuma	本	3	追撃刀	Tsugekito
4	後	Ushiro	4	浮雲	Ukigumo	の	4	斜刀	Shato
5	八重垣	Yaegaki	5	嵐	Arashi	型	5	四方刀 No.1	Shihoto No.1
6	受流	Ukenagashi	6	岩波	Iwanami		6	四方刀 No.2	Shihoto No.2
7	介錯	Kaishaku	7	鱗返	Urokogaeshi		7	斬突刀	Zantotsuto
8	附込	Tsukekomi	8	浪返	Namigaeshi	奥	8	前敵逆刀	Zentekigyakuto
9	月影	Tsukikage	9	瀧落	Takiotoshi	の	9	多敵刀	Tatekito
10	追風	Oikaze	10	真向	Makko	型	10	後敵逆刀	Kotekigyakuto
11	抜打	Nukiuchi					11	後敵抜打	Kotekinukuchi
鞘の内 居逢の生命								
和歌								

Handwritten in Japanese script and western characters, this is page 1 of a list of every kata in the Muso Jikiden Eishin Ryu system (it is marked 'Eishin Ryu Menkyo Kaiden') given to my father by Keiji Tose.

19

Takenouchi Ryu

*The headmaster of Takenouchi Ryu with
British Jujutsu instructor Allan Tattersall*

While all Koryu taught a variety of martial arts (Kenjutsu, Jujutsu, Bojutsu, Sojutsu - whatever the case may be), the Takenouchi Ryu is synonymous with Jujutsu and is said to be Japan's oldest specific Jujutsu school. That is not say Takenouchi Ryu always uses the phrase Jujutsu. It also uses 'Hade' which may be related to the term Hakuda used by Yoshin Ryu, Torite, and Koshi no Mawari. Tekenouchi Ryu was established by Takenouchi Nakatsukasadayu Hisamori in around 1530 and almost 500 years later it remains in the Takenouchi family. According to the records of the family, Takenouchi Nakatsukasadayu Hisamori learned his skills from the Yamabushi (mountain warrior monks) while praying to the god Atago. The skills he learnt were called 'Shinden torite gokajo.'

Serge Mol (*Classical Fighting Arts of Japan*) writes: *'The exact meaning of the term Hade is a little obscure, but technically speaking it was one system for attacking the vital points of the body. This term can be found in transmission scrolls of the Takenouchi Ryu... Hade is sometimes also called Kempo Taijutsu.'* Takenouchi Ryu also used the phrase 'Koshi no Mawari.' Mol writes: *'From the Koshi no Mawari a new system was developed in which the use of short swords was not required. Instead one would attack the anatomically weak points of the body with atemi, in order to weaken the enemy before using nagewaza.*

20

Knowledge of these vulnerable points, called Kyusho or also tsubo was passed on by word of mouth.'

In addition to Jujutsu, Torite and the other previously discussed grappling and striking systems, Takenouchi Ryu also includes Kenjutsu (fencing), Iaido (sword drawing), Naginata (halberd), Tessen (fan) and Hojo (rope tying). Takenouchi Ryu grants five certificates of competency. The first was Tassha, the next in common with Daito Ryu was Mokuroku, followed by Jiro and then finally Menkyo and Inka.

Because of its age and reputation, a number of other schools trace their origins back to Takenouchi Ryu. These include Fusen Ryu and Araki Ryu.

After the 8th head of Takenouchi Ryu, the lineage broke into two branches, the Soke's line which is presently headed by Takenouchi Toichiro Hisamune (the 14th Soke who focusses on the Torite teachings), and the Sodenke line which is currently headed by the 13th generation head of Koshi no Mawari teachings Takenouchi Tojuro Hisatake. In addition to the Soke and Sodenke lines there are other lines claiming a Takenouchi Ryu lineage, including the Bitchuden line which was developed by Takeuchi Seidaiyu Masatsugu. The Bitchuden branch is based in Kyoto where the 16th head of the school, Kancho Ono Yotaro Shinjin, runs the Choufukan Dojo.

There is an official branch of the Bitchuden branch of Takenouchi Ryu in Yorkshire. The school writes: *'Shoufukan, the name of our Dojo, opened in autumn 2007 in Mirfield under Anna Seabourne Sensei who returned earlier that year from twelve years studying martial arts in Japan.'* The school describes the training as follows: *'Students train through kata or "forms", often repeating the basic movements many times. Beginners start with the bo (six foot staff) and learning how to fall safely, before moving on to blocks, throws, locks and releases, then weapons such as the bokuto (wooden sword), jo (short staff) and kogusoku.'*

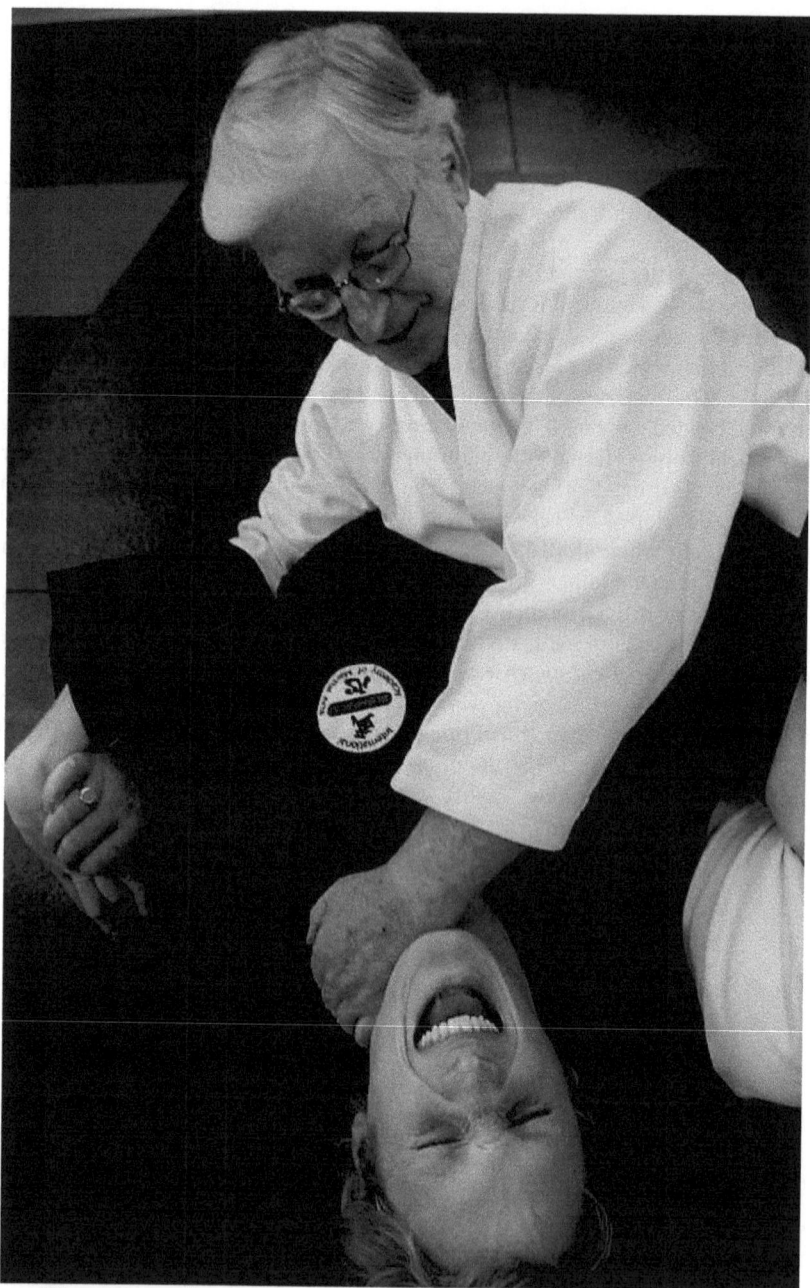

Allan Tattersall with the author in 2007. Tattersall Hanshi is one of few westerners to have trained in both Takenouchi Ryu and Muso Jikiden Eishin Ryu in Japan, and he was granted his own Ryu-ha name by the Dai Nippon Butokukai of which he was the UK director for many rears.

Yagyu Shingan Ryu

Yagyu Shingan Ryu is a very difficult Ryuha to comprehend because its origins seem to defy logic. Today there are two main branches of Yagyu Shingan Ryu, one known as 'Yagyu Shingan Ryu Heiho' and the other as 'Yagyu Shingan Ryu Taijutsu'. Stylistically these two branches are very similar. The Heiho (meaning strategy) branch is more gymnastic, resembling in parts acrobatic Wushu, and cites Takenaga Hayato as its founder. The Taijutsu branch has more of a feeling of simulating armour-clad movements and cites Araki Mataemon as its founder. Aside from their differences the branches are clearly related and both branch founders, Takenaga and Araki, seem to have been students of Ushu Tatewaki of Shindo Ryu, and both were given permission to use the word 'Yagyu' by the famous Yagyu Munenori. However, both styles also seem to converge with one Koyama Samon, who moved to Edo (Tokyo), thereby establishing the new Edo line (Taijutsu) as distinct from the previous Sendai line (Heiho).

The author demonstrating Yawara

Today there are at least four Japanese masters claiming to be Soke of Yagyu Shingan Ryu. These include Shimazu Kenji (Chikuosha branch of Sendai/Heiho line), Hoshi Konio II (Ryushinkan branch of Sendai/Heiho line), Kajitsuka Yasushi (Taijutsu or Edo line) and various inheritors of Jun Osano and Sato Kinbei discussed below. Heiho branch founder Takenaga Hayato was already a practitioner of Shindo Ryu, Shuza Ryu and Toda Ryu when he established himself as a teacher of Shingan Ryu. Takenaga met Yagyu Munenori, the head of Yagyu Shinkage Ryu (a style of Kenjutsu), who allowed Takenaga to use the Yagyu name. This is a significant gesture, as Yagyu Shinkage Ryu was the official style taught to only the highest in society, including the Shogun themselves. Thus 'licensing' use of the Yagyu name was a huge seal of approval. It is worth re-iterating that Yagyu Shingan Ryu was mostly a style of Jujutsu and Yagyu Shinkage Ryu was mostly a sword school. The two have little in common stylistically.

Following Takenaga Hayato the tradition was passed on to Yoshikawa Ichiroemon, then to Ito Kyuzaburo, then to Koyama Samon, who traveled to Edo and became the headmaster of the Edo line. From Koyama Samon, the Sendai (Heiho) line passed through Aizawa Tadanoshin Token, Chiba Yoshikazu and Satake Shinnosuke and then to Kato Gonzo. Sato Kinbei studied under Suzuki Sensaku, student of Suzuki Heikichi and Kato Hikokichi, who were both students of Takahashi Hikohichi, and he, under Hoshi Sadakichi, a student of Kato Gonzo. Sato's daughter wrote: *'It was 1950 when my father Sato Kinbei received his license to teach Yagyu Shingan Ryu, just after he returned from the war in China. According to him, Yagyu Shingan Ryu is different from other forms of Jujutsu in terms of its practicality on the field of battle and its unrivaled fierceness and ability to kill the enemy. It is said that the experienced practitioner can shatter an enemy arm with one blow.'*

Shimazu Kenji and Hoshi Kunio II also trained under lineages which trace back to Kato Gonzo. Jun Osano claims to hold Menkyo Kaiden in nine Ryuha including Yagyu Shingan Ryu, Asayama Ichiden Ryu, Shinto Munen Ryu and Nitto Ichi Ryu. He held an 8th dan in Nihon Jujutsu under Kokusai Budoin and was a Shihan of the Nihon Jujutsu division along with Minoru Mochizuki and Shizuya Sato.

In terms of the Taijutsu line, both Morihei Ueshiba (founder of Aikido) and Jigoro Kano (founder of Judo) studied this school with the sixth Soke, Goto Saburo, and the seventh Soke, Ohshima Masateru, respectively. In *Karate Jutsu* I looked at the possibility that present day Yagyu Shingan Ryu had a common ancestor with Shuri family Karate. Not only are the Yagyu Shingan Ryu forms reminiscent of the Karate form Naihanchi, including its signature 'returning wave' step, but Yagyu Shingan Ryu also taught the use of farming implements as weapons. Yagyu Shingan Ryu also uses solo kata rather like Karate kata in addition to the usual two man sets. Its circular, flowing strikes are reminiscent of the Chinese art of Hsing-I Chuan and the art eschews the usual hip throws and pins that dominate Judo and modern Jujutsu. Another interesting factor is that within the Yagyu Shingan Ryu was a method called Totte no Jutsu, a term linguistically similar to the Okinawan Tote Jutsu.

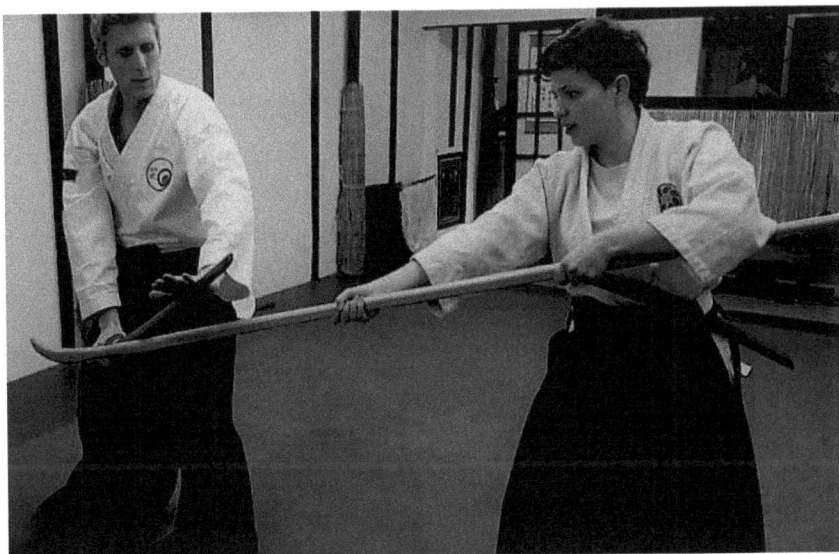

The author demonstrating katana defences against Naginata.

Yagyu Shingan Ryu was created to be a battlefield art with a large comprehensive curriculum of weapons, and grappling techniques for use both while armoured and unarmoured, training several arts, including Yawara (Jujutsu), quarterstaff fighting (Bojutsu), glaive fighting (Naginatajutsu), sword drawing techniques (Iaijutsu), and sword fighting (Kenjutsu). The unarmed aspects of Yagyu Shingan Ryu included Suburi (Suhada Jujutsu, atemi), Torite no Jutsu – Torikata no Yawara (restraints), Totte no Jutsu (escapes), Kogusoku Totte (grappling with armour and shortswords), and Gyoi dori (defence against Iaijutsu). Kobudo agricultural style weapons of Yagyu Shingan Ryu included Hananejibo (a Jutte originally used to control horses), Bashin (a double edge knife used to bleed horses), and Jingama (Kama sickle).

Tenjin Shinyo Ryu

*With thanks to Lee Masters and Paul Masters both
Menkyo Kaiden in Tenjin Shinyo Ryu*

Tenjin Shinyo Ryu is one of Japan's cultural heritages and is recognised as a Koryu. Tenjin Shinyo Ryu emerged around the Tokugawa Bakufu period and was founded by Iso Mataemon Ryukansai Minamoto No Masatari. The origin of the school's teaching came from two older styles of Jujutsu. The first was Yoshin Ryu, founded in the late Tokugawa period (c.1660) by Akiyama Shirobei Yoshitoki. The second was Shin No Shinto Ryu, which was created by Yamamoto Tamizaemon Hidehaya (c.1780). Both of these schools' teachings have been preserved and perpetuated within Tenjin Shinyo Ryu.

The history of the school's foundation is to be found in one of its most treasured documents called the Tai-I-Roku. The Tai-I-Roku states that the founder of Tenjin Shinyo Ryu was Iso Mataemon Ryukansai Minamoto No Masatari. He was born in Matsuzaka prefecture of Ise. His birth name was Okayama Hachiroji Masatari. When he was a child he was very interested in Bu-Jutsu (martial arts) and at the age of 15 he travelled to Kyoto to become a student of Hitotsu Yanagi Oribe of the Yoshin Ryu. After the death of his teacher he then went on to study Shin No Shinto Ryu under Homma Jouemon. After six years he learnt the Okuden 'deeper teachings' of this system.

Following the study of Shin No Shinto Ryu, Iso Mataemon embarked on a Musha Shugyo – travelling around the country seeking contest matches with official instructors of each feudal domain. Throughout the three years spent on

26

this discipline he remained undefeated. During this period he visited the village of Kusatsu Ormi of Shiga Ken prefecture where he stayed and taught Jujutsu. At this time it happened that a group of villains threatened the residents there. Iso decided to protect them and, aided by his able student Nishimura, he waged a savage fight against more than one hundred adversaries. Iso and his student defeated their opponents and from this experience he realised the importance of Shin No Ate – striking the body's physiological weak points. Following this experience Iso travelled to northern Kyoto where he undertook Seishin Tan Ren – a series of spiritual and physical exercises for forging the mind and body, at the Kitano Tenmangu shrine. It is here that he named his ryu Tenjin Shinyo Ryu.

Iso Mataemon took the word Tenjin in honour of Sugawara Michizane, who is enshrined at the Kitano Tenmangu shrine. Iso Mataemon then combined the words Shin and Yo, the two Kobudo styles he had studied previously. During his meditation at Kitano, Iso Mataemon became enlightened by the willow tree and how its branches yielded against the strong winds without breaking and then returned with a powerful whipping force. From this enlightenment he was able to create new techniques.

Iso Mataemon opened a dojo in Otamagaike, now known as the Kanda area of Tokyo. He also taught for the Togugawa Shogunate at the Kobusho – the official training institute of military arts. Both classes proved extremely popular and it is said that Tenjin Shinyo Ryu was the most famous ryu at that time (around 1860) with more than 5000 students. Iso Mataemon Ryukansai Minamoto No Masatari died in 1863 at the age of 76.

Tenjin Shinyo Ryu makimono

Within the curriculum of Tenjin Shinyo Ryu there are 124 kata keiko – or form training. These are divided into five sections and taught by natural progression, at five different levels and by five transmission licences. The first

27

two are Shoden and Chuden - first and middle level - and come in the form of Kiri Gami Menjo, or cut paper licence. The remaining three Mokuroku, catalogue, Menkyo – licence to teach and Menkyo Kaiden – full licence of transmission, come in the form of makimono – rolled scroll.

When the monjin (initiated practitioner) of Tenjin Shinyo Ryu reaches the Menkyo level he is regarded as being a correct person to start to teach the esoteric, cosmological concepts of Tenjin Shinyo Ryu. Within these concepts are the Sanmitsu or three secrets or three mysteries. The Sanmitsu has its origins both in Ko Shinto and Shingon Buddhism. The Sanmitsu comprises of three principles:

1) Mandara – visualisation
2) Inkei – hand seal
3) Mantra – special word sounds

These three principles are usually practised simultaneously for the purpose of unifying the mind, body and speech in order to empty the mind of all distractions and be able to focus with absolute clarity. Mandara uses the principle of visualising sacred symbols, mystical illustrations and deity forms, Inkei or Ketsu-in uses various hand and finger formations, and Mantra uses vocal intonations, known as kotodama in Shinto or mantras in Shingon Buddhism. The above is a broad definition of these principles. Another term which embraces the above is called Jumon, which properly refers to a mystical incantation or talisman for health, protection and power. Through the study and application of these principles it is believed that the Tenjin Shinyo Ryu monjin can eradicate fear and develop a psychological mindset likened to 'Muga Mushin': no ego, no self, no mind during combat. At the level of Menkyo, these principles are applied in the Gokui Jodan Tachiai katas – ultimate upper level standing forms, of which there are ten. For example, in the Gokui Jodan kata 'Oh Goroshi' – Big Kill, there is the principle of San Mi Atari, three body strike. Within this principle is also the principle of the Sanmitsu, conjointly the utilisation of both these principles in Tenjin Shinyo Ryu is known as 'Seishi Ron' and depicts the three combat phases of Zenshin, Tsushin and Zanshin. These three phases of combat in esoteric terms represent the 'Shu Kongo' – the deity holding a vajra.

Pictures from the kata 'Oh Goroshi' demonstrated by Menkyo Kaiden holders Paul Masters Shike and his son Lee Masters:

This deity and the deity Naraenkengo are considered to be guardians known as Nio – two kings. In Buddhism they are usually considered as deities of extraordinary strength, and their statues are often placed at temple gates with one of them keeping its mouth wide open and the other keeping its mouth tightly closed. Their presence is to stop evil and let virtue pass. These two deities are the manifestation of the Sente Kannon Bosatsu, the one with eleven heads and a thousand arms. This deity is mentioned in the Tai-I-Roku, a very important teaching document of the Tenjin Shinyo Ryu, coming from the Soke, Iso Mataemon. The original Sanskrit term for this deity is Samantemukha, whose original meaning was '*The one who turns his face to all directions*'. This 'all directions' represents the eight cardinal directions and the directions toward heaven and earth. So the full correct name for this deity in Japan is 'Juichimen Senju Kannon Bosatsu', eleven heads and a thousand arms. The number one thousand indicates numerous or infinite. The sculptures or images of the Senju Kannon usually have 42 arms, twenty on its right side and twenty on its left, with one additional pair placed in the 'Gassho In' position in front of the breast. Each arm is believed to represent twenty five arms; thereby the total number becomes one thousand. In the Tai-I-Roku of Tenjin Shinyo Ryu there is reference that relates to the mind skill of the Sente Kannon in relation to the control and use of ki. It advises to fill oneself with ki, in other words to allow the ki to permeate the whole body, from the top of your head to the tips of your fingers and toes and to let your body and spirit of mind to repose correctly and calmly so that you do not reveal even one opening. The Tai-I-Roku gives an example of this by referring to the Sente Kannon: '*The thousand armed goddess has only one mind, but that mind extends to move a thousand arms, each in its own way. Should her mind incline too much in any one direction then inevitably some of the arms would cease their movement and having a thousand arms would become useless.*' This statement also represents the unity of the Tenjin Shinyo Ryu concept of 'Shi Ki Ryuoku' – will, energy, power.

British Jujutsu Pre-History

The early days of Judo [Public Domain]

Jujutsu is thought to have begun its development in the Sengoku period (c. 1467 – c. 1600) of Japanese history. Martial arts in neighbouring states like Okinawa or China were developing around striking techniques, which would have been largely ineffective against Samurai in armour on the battlefield, and so early Jujutsu consisted mainly of grappling, choking, throwing and joint locks. At this time however the term Jujutsu was not being used. It was not until the 17th century, during the Edo (or Tokugawa) period, when the term Jujutsu was introduced as a generic one to capture all grappling systems and techniques. The Edo period of Japan (1603 – 1868) was a time of relative peace. The role of the Samurai was changing and there was little need for armour or weapons, and the evolution of the unarmed combat accelerated, with Jujutsu Ryu proliferating to the extent that towards the end of the Edo period there were more than 300 Jujutsu Ryu.

In 1877, an 18 year old called Jigoro Kano at Tokyo Imperial University started training in Tenjin Shinyo Ryu with teacher and bonesetter Fukuda Hachinosuke. Two years later, in 1879, Kano took part in a demonstration given for former US president Ulysses S. Grant, along with Fukuda Hachinosuke, another teacher, 3rd generation head-master Iso Mataemon Masatomo, and student Godai Ryusaku. Following Fukuda Hachinosuke's death Kano continued to learn with Iso Mataemon Masatomo. Kano was of small stature and he realised that in order to generate a fighting style that would be effective against all comers.

Jigoro Kano (1860 – 1938) the founder of Kodokan Judo.
[Public Domain]

he would need to utilise elements from other ryu. Thus, when his teacher Iso died in 1881 Kano started to learn Kito Ryu with Iikubo Tsunetoshi.

Kano then started to develop his own style, utilising the best aspects of multiple styles to make the most effective system. In 1882 Kano Jujutsu, or Judo, was established, which would become known as Kodokan Judo. In 1888, Kano and a Reverend Thomas Lindsay delivered a lecture at the British Embassy in Tokyo called 'Jiujutsu: The Old Samurai Art of Fighting without Weapons'. Kano opens the lecture with a definition of Jujutsu by stating: *'The word Jujutsu may be translated freely as "the art of gaining victory by yielding or pliancy." Originally, the name seems to have been applied to what may best be described as the art of fighting without weapons, although in some cases short weapons were used against opponents fighting with long weapons. Although it seems to resemble wrestling, yet it differs materially from wrestling as practiced in*

England, its main principle being not to match strength with strength, but to gain victory by yielding to strength.' Kano actively promoted Kodokan Judo, firstly throughout Japan, and then globally by sending his Kodokan Judo experts abroad. By the age of 25 Kano had become a Professor of Political Science and Economics. Kano would later become a politician and subsequently serve on the International Olympic Committee.

Mataemon Tanabe (1869 – 1942) of the Fusen Ryu
[Public Domain]

Another ryu of importance to British Jujutsu was established by Motsugai Takeda (1795 – 1867), who founded the Fusen Ryu. Fusen Ryu specialised in newaza or ground fighting. In the late 1800s Jujutsu schools were being dominated by Kano Jujutsu/Judo. In 1881 the Fusen Ryu gained notoriety when their top master Mataemon Tanabe (1869 – 1942) defeated Takisaburo Tobari from the Kodokan in a challenge match, mainly thanks to his vastly superior ground work. A result of this was the incorporation of the newaza of Fusen Ryu into Kano Jujutsu/Kodokan Judo. Mataemon Tanabe started learning Jujutsu from his father at the age of 9, and by 17 was Menkyo Kaiden. Growing up, Tanabe would take on all opponents, often much bigger than himself. Although Tanabe was never formally part of the Kodokan of Kano he did teach at the Dai Nippon Butoku Kai (see below) for many years, where he was made Kyoshi and subsequently Hanshi in Judo.

In 1885 in Kyoto the Dai Nippon Butoku Kai (DNBK, Greater Japan Martial Virtue Society) was established under the supporting authority of the national government and the endorsement of the Meiji Emperor to promote and standardise the martial disciplines of Japan. It was the first official martial arts institution and premier governing body of Japan. The Prince Komatsunomiya Akihito Shinno, Commander of the Imperial Army, served as the first Supreme Chair, or Sosai, endowing the DNBK with prestige. In 1899, the Butokuden (Hall of Martial Virtues) was rebuilt, again in Kyoto. This was the first martial arts institution of its kind, a governing body of sorts attended by the nation's leading experts in all disciplines of martial arts, including the premier Jujutsu teachers of the time from leading ryu, including Mataemon Tanabe of Fusen Ryu, and Jigoro Kano of Kodokan Judo.

Dai Nippon Butokukai badges issued 1898 – 1945.
[Picture: David Brough]

William Adams (1564 –1620), known in Japanese as Miura Anjin or 'Samurai William', was famously the first 'English Samurai.'

In 1600 he was the first Briton to reach Japan during a five-ship expedition for the Dutch East India Company. Adams was the first ever (of a very few) Western Samurai and became a key advisor to the Shogun Tokugawa Ieyasu. In 1614, Adams stayed in Okinawa from 27 December 1614 until May 1615.

In 1616 Japan banned trade with foreigners. The only exception was that traders in Nagasaki bay were entitled to import from China. The powerful Dutch East India Trading Company got round the ban in 1634 by partitioning off part of Nagasaki with ditches, to in effect make their own island called Dejima.

In 1667 the first Swedish book about Japan and China was written by two Swedish sailors who had been there on Dutch ships. In 1731 the Swedish East India Trading Company was created, inspired by the likes of the Dutch East India Company to trade with the Far East as far as Japan and Guangzhou, and in 1745 the Swedish ship Gotheborg was famously sunk on the way back from China.

As well as importing spices, Sweden was also exporting steel to Japan. Swedish steel from railway sleepers was used to make the legendary Japanese sword. The best 'mill steel' gendaito are made from mid-19th century railway tracks that were manufactured from Swedish steel and exported to Japan. Swedish steel has been highly prized for its excellence and purity.

In 1775 Swedish physician Carl Thunberg moved to Dejima near Okinawa. In 1776 he met the Shogun in Edo, and in 1779 he returned to Sweden. Thunberg was a student of the earlier Swedish physician Carl Nilsson.

A French naval expedition under Captain Fornier-Duplan onboard Alcmène visited Okinawa on April 28, 1844. Trade was denied, but Father Forcade was left behind with a Chinese translator, named Auguste Ko. Forcade and Ko remained in the Ameku Shogen-ji Temple near the port of Tomari.

After a period of one year, on May 1, 1846, the French ship Sabine, commanded by Guérin, arrived, soon followed by La Victorieuse, commanded by Rigault de Genouilly, and Cléopâtre, under Admiral Cécille.

The Ryukyu court in Shuri (now part of Naha) complained in early 1847 about the presence of the French missionaries, who had to be removed in 1848.

France would have no further contacts with Okinawa for the next 7 years, until news came that Commodore Perry had obtained an agreement with the islands on July 11, 1854, following his treaty with Japan.

Commodore Perry arrives in Okinawa [Public Doman]

Subsequently sailors developed a style of boxing based on what they had studied called Chausson, which may be a forerunner to Savate, which in turn influenced some of the early British Jujutsu pioneers.

The Chinese Martial Studies website states: 'A precursor of modern French Boxing called "Chausson" is said to have been popular with French sailors in Marseilles and was later adopted by the French Navy. This style of kickboxing featured higher kicks and open hand slaps rather than punches.

'These facts have been expanded upon to introduce a nautical element into the modern mythology of French Boxing. Some commentators claim that these arts were actually shaped by their origins on the cramped spaces of a ship. They assert that the hands were left open so that they could steady a sailor on the deck of a pitching ship. Of course it could also be that punching someone in the face with a closed fist without boxing gloves is not always a great idea (ergo the frequency with which a wide variety of global fighting systems use open hand strikes). Such traditions will of course sound vaguely familiar to students of the southern Chinese martial arts, which are also sometimes said to have been shaped by their nautical precursors.'

Although the beginnings of Savate came from the Paris slums, formalisation of a fighting style using predominantly kicking, rather than punching (as was the case in English boxing at the time), began with the French Navy developing Chausson— meaning 'slipper,' in reference to the sailors' footwear at the time. Chausson soon became a local street game about Marseille, Aubagne and Toulon and was named jeu Marseillais (game from Marseilles).

During the Napoleonic Wars the average Frenchman's exposure to Chausson increased as they were conscripted into fighting, which served to spread the fighting style and perhaps was influential in exposing Chausson and Savate practitioners to each other. At the time both Savate and Chausson did not involve striking the opponent with the fists, probably due to fist fighting being outlawed by the French government. Instead, they preferred to use open-hand techniques such as slapping to defend against kicks and to strike opponents. Again, another influence on Savate came during the Napoleonic Wars with French prisoners of war being exposed to boxing by their British captors, but it was not until much later that boxing made its way into the fighting style.

Savate began to be regulated with the opening of the first salle (official training school) by the famous instructor Michel Casseux (1794-1869), also known by his nickname of le Pisseux. Disallowing such techniques as head butting, eye gouging and grappling, Cassaux created a system of Savate and added la canne (cane fencing), calling it the 'Art of Savate.' He went on to teach many famous members of French society.

The first real exposure to Jujutsu for the British was to those living and working in Japan in the late 1800s. One of the first British pioneers of Jujutsu was a man called Ernest John Harrison. Harrison, born in Manchester in 1873, excelled at boxing and wrestling growing up, which fuelled an interest in the fighting arts. Aged just 19 years he left the UK for firstly Canada, then the USA, before arriving in Yokohama, Japan, in 1887, where he found employment as reporter and news editor for the English language newspaper the *Japan Herald*.

At the age of 23 Harrison was able to enrol in the Tenjin Shinyo Ryu Jujutsu dojo of Ryoshinsai Hagiwara. The Japanese were reluctant to teach the 'Gaijin' or foreigners the secrets of Jujutsu, and so it is a testament to Harrison's immersion and adoption of Japanese culture and life that he was able to do this. Harrison would later move to Tokyo, where he would learn Kodokan Judo, and where, in 1911, he would become the first Westerner to achieve a black belt. The first foreigner to enrol at the Kodokan was a Major H.M. Hughes, on the 14th August, 1893, though further information on Major Hughes is lacking.

Another British Jujutsu pioneer was Harry H. Hunter (more on him later). Harry Hunter was a sailor in the British Navy and in 1904 was based in Yokohama to teach gunnery to Japanese ratings. In a newspaper interview in 1939 Hunter said the inspiration for learning Jujutsu was seeing a little Japanese boy flooring a big British sailor. Hunter appears to have been less accepted than Harrison as a Jujutsu student as he claimed the Japanese instructors wouldn't teach him all the Jujutsu techniques. He therefore learnt much by observation. It is not clear what style Hunter learnt but as Harrison had been accepted into Tenjin Shinyo Ryu as a Gaijin in Yokohama, and given that Tenjin Shinyo Ryu was the most widely taught system, and Hunter was also in Yokohama, it seems reasonable to suggest that Tenjin Shinyo Ryu was what Hunter learnt. Hunter would later return to the UK promoting himself as the 'Jujutsu champion of Europe'. He worked as a policeman in Lancashire, also training various police forces in Jujutsu, before moving to Canada in 1929, where he also trained the police in self-defence. In 1927 he published the book *Super Jujitsu* which would have been an early Gendai form of Jujutsu.

Another Westerner to encounter Jujutsu was Patrick Lafcadio Hearn (1850 – 1904). Lafcadio Hearn was an author and was best known for his books about Japan. Hearn lived in Japan from 1890 and it is clear Jujutsu left a lasting impression. Writing about Jujutsu in *Out of the East* (1895) Hearn writes: *'What Western brain could have elaborated this strange teaching, -never to oppose force by force, but only direct and utilize the power of attack; to overthrow the enemy solely through his own strength, -to vanquish him solely by his own efforts? Surely none! The Western mind appears to work in straight lines; the Oriental, in wonderful curves and circles. Yet how fine a symbolism of Intelligence as a means of foiling brute force! Much more than a science of defense in this jiujitsu: it is a philosophical system; it is an economical system; it is an ethical system, (indeed, I may say that a very large part of jiujitsu training is purely moral); and it is, above all, the expression of a racial genius as yet but faintly perceived by these Powers who dream of further aggrandizement in the East.'*

Picture of Harry Hunter in training gear from his book 'Super Jujitsu.' Note the dark (presumably black) shorts and broad sash. This pre-dates the modern Judo style uniform [Public domain, 1927]

Jujutsu Comes to the UK

Portrait of Edward William Barton-Wright
[Reproduced with permission from the Bartitsu Society]

Perhaps the first demonstration of Jujutsu in the UK occurred in 1892 when Takashima Shidachi gave a lecture on Jujutsu in London for the Japan Society. Part of this lecture was a practical demonstration (in dinner suits) by Takashima Shidachi, using Daigoro Goh as his assistant, who was the chancellor of the Japanese consulate general and secretary of the Japan Society.

Another early reference to Jujutsu was also in an 1892 edition of an illustrated monthly publication called *The Idler*. The story was about Inugami Gunbei, of Kyushin Ryu, who defeated a famous wrestler called Onogawa Kisaburo and became his teacher.

These events likely set the scene for another real pioneer of Jujutsu in the UK; a martial arts enthusiast named Edward William Barton-Wright.

Barton-Wright was born on the 8th of November 1860, in India, to an English father and a Scottish mother, and where his father was working as a railway engineer. Barton-Wright's family returned to England and he was educated in France and Germany. With a life-long passion for martial arts, it was while working in Japan as an antimony smelting specialist for the E.H. Hunter Company in Kobe (c 1895 – 1898) that Barton-Wright studied Jujutsu of the

Shinden-Fudo Ryu under Terajima Kuniichiro in Kobe, and Kano Jujutsu with Jigoro Kano in Tokyo.

Upon returning to the UK in 1898 Barton-Wright tapped into the mood of the period, which was driven by a growing fear of street violence, a fascination with Japanese culture, and an interest in physical recreation, and created Bartitsu, 'The Gentlemanly Art of Self-Defence', which was a portmanteau of his own surname and Jujitsu. Prior to opening his school Barton-Wright wrote several articles for *Pearson's Magazine*. The first of these articles was in March of 1899 and was called 'The New Art of Self Defence.' In this article Barton-Wright describes and demonstrates a number of self defence moves in pictures with a Japanese Jujutsuka – the preparation of these pictures prior to his return to the UK suggests that Barton-Wright fully intended to develop teaching aids upon his return. A footnote in this first article describes a 'performance' by Barton-Wright where he fought a champion of Cumberland and Westmoreland Wrestling, a Mr. Chipchase. According to the editor, using his new method of self defence, Barton-Wright made light work of Mr. Chipchase. It was this performance that won over the first sceptical editorial office to publish Barton-Wright's article. The second article was published in *Pearson's Magazine* only a few months later and sees the first mention of the name 'Bartitsu'. At the end of the second article Barton-Wright states his intention to open a school of self defence and describes another ten self defence moves. One of the described moves is how to deal with a boxing attack, possibly representing a first adaption of Jujutsu to a Western fighting style.

Barton-Wright opened the Bartitsu School of Arms and Physical Culture in 1900 at 67b Shaftesbury Avenue in London. Bartitsu was not one martial art, but an eclectic collection of systems that Barton-Wright thought important for effective self-defence. To deliver classes in the various styles Barton-Wright invited specialist instructors to teach at his club. These included Pierre Vigny, who specialised in French Savate (kickboxing) and la canne (cane fighting), the Swiss wrestler Armand Cherpillod, and fencing experts such as Captain Alfred Hutton. Barton-Wright would also teach. However, to deliver the Jujutsu classes further Barton-Wright took the important step of inviting several Japanese Jujutsuka (practitioners of Jujutsu) to teach at his school. It was the invitation of these Japanese Jujutsuka that was to transform Jujutsu in the UK, and around the world.

Seemingly through correspondence with his colleague Jigoro Kano, Barton-Wright coordinated the arrival of three Japanese Jujutsuka in 1900. These were the brothers Kaneo Tani and the teenage Yukio Tani, and Seizo Yamamoto. The Tani brothers were students of Mataemon Tanabe of Fusen Ryu Jujutsu, who was closely associated with the dojo of Yotaro Handa, while Yamamoto was a student of Handa. Whilst the Tani brothers and Yamamoto were brought to teach Jujutsu at the Bartitsu club, Barton-Wright also wanted to make money on the music hall circuit performing demonstrations and taking on prize fighters and wrestlers. Kaneo Tani and Yamamoto refused to take part in demonstrations, complaining it was an undignified use of Jujutsu, and promptly returned to Japan. On December the 29th 1900 the magazine *Black and White Budget* published an article about a visit to the Bartitsu club called 'The Latest Fashionable Pastime.' Pictured in this article are Pierre Vigny demonstrating cane fighting and Savate. Also published is a picture of two Japanese Jujutsuka. The caption accompanying the picture of the Jujutsuka states 'Two very clever Japanese wrestlers who exhibit at the club, but who will not appear in public owing to their high caste.' From this statement we can infer that the two Japanese wrestlers in the picture are Kaneo Tani and Seizo Yamamoto. This article also gives insight into the Physical Culture aspect of the Bartitsu club, including pictures of an electric light massaging machine to cure neuralgia, and light therapy to cure diphtheria!

In 1901 Barton-Wright wrote again in *Pearson's Magazine*. This time Barton-Wright presented two articles on 'Self Defence With a Walking Stick.' The first article refers to how the walking stick defences of Vigny were assimilated into Bartitsu and taught at his School of Arms and Physical Culture, and also includes a defence against a boxer. The second article has further defences including 'How to Use a Walking Stick as a Weapon in a Crowd.'

Following the return of Kaneo Tani and Yamamoto to Japan in 1900 Barton-Wright recruited another young Japanese Jujutsuka called Sadakazu Uyenishi. Sadakazu Uyenishi was born in Osaka, Japan, in 1880. His father, Kichibe Uyenishi, was a famous athlete, noted for his unusual physical strength and skill at kenjutsu, horsemanship, swimming and sumo wrestling. Sadakazu Uyenishi trained at the dojo of Yataro Handa in Osaka. Before 1897 the Handa dojo was associated with Tenjin Shinyo Ryu. However the Handa dojo that opened in 1897 focussed on a style called Daito Ryu, not the same as the well-known style discussed above of Takeda Sokaku, but an off-shoot of Sekiguchi Ryu. In 1898 Mataemon Tanabe came to teach at Handa's dojo, where he innovated with his newaza techniques. Within a couple of years the Handa dojo was known for competitive newaza. Uyenishi was said to have been a champion in Japan. Like the young Yukio Tani, Sadakazu Uyenishi had no qualms about appearing on the music hall circuit.

At this time Jujutsu was proving to be very popular, and coincided with the emergence of a style of wrestling called Catch as Catch Can (or simply Catch) which developed in the UK. Some years ago I interviewed a Catch wrestling coach in Wigan who explained how Catch arose. It was originally a way for coal miners to settle disputes. They would come above ground and wrestle on the shale. Catch wrestling was an unforgiving sport and allowed any part of the body to be seized - catch whatever you can!

Matches between Catch wrestlers and Jujutsuka were very popular and Tani and Uyenishi were a revelation on the music hall scene, with audiences marvelling at their skills. However, things were more difficult at the Bartitsu club and it struggled. Student William Garrud later remarked that he thought this was because of membership and training fees being too expensive. Ultimately, things came to a head when Tani and Barton-Wright fell out over money and had a fight. Barton-Wright later claimed he won the fight with Tani, although this is debatable. Tani, Barton-Wright's main attraction, left the Bartitsu club, which shortly closed thereafter in 1903.

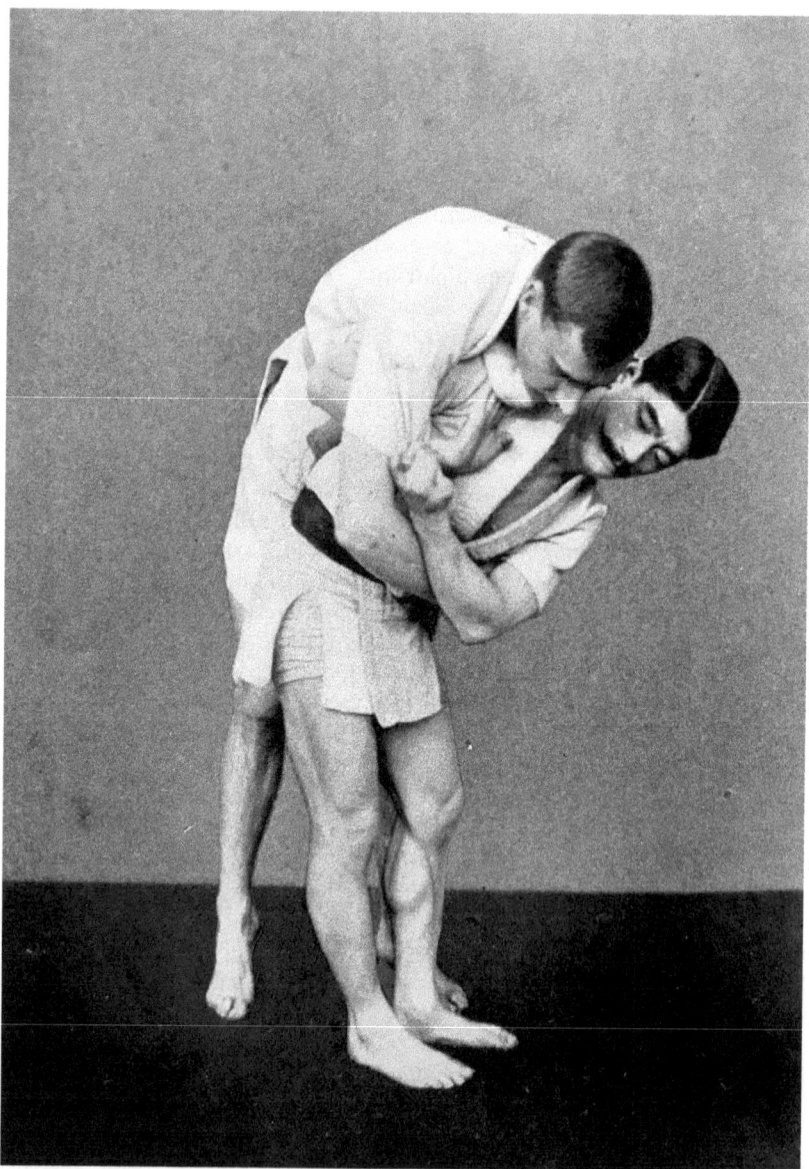

The formidable Raku Uyenishi who may have influenced British Jujutsu more than any other Japanese master [Public Domain]

Barton-Wright never practised martial arts again, and spent the rest of his life pursuing various other ventures before dying penniless in 1951 at the age of 90. He is buried in a pauper's grave at the Kingston Cemetery in Surrey. Bartitsu was mostly forgotten about, eclipsed by the popularity of Jujutsu, except for an obscure reference in Sir Arthur Conan Doyle's 1902 Sherlock Holmes story *The Adventure of the Empty House*. 100 years later, in 2002, after scholars had uncovered some of Barton-Wright's magazine articles, the author and Bartitsu enthusiast Will Thomas established the Bartitsu Society, initially to research Bartitsu, and subsequently to continue the martial arts cross-training experiments pioneered by Barton-Wright.

When the Bartitsu club closed, la canne and Savate expert Pierre Vigny opened a school in London in 1903 based at number 18 Berner Street under the patronage of Grand Duke Michael of Russia, and became the director of the New School of Self-Defence and Fencing Academy. Vigny was born in Paris, France in 1866. Vigny's method of la canne would become heavily influenced by his experiences at the Bartitsu club and he is best remembered for establishing a unique style of stick fighting which also used walking sticks and umbrellas. Indeed Vigny's wife also taught at the Berner Street school, offering ladies classes in the use of the parasol and the steel-spiked umbrella. In 1912 Vigny moved to Geneva to establish a new self-defence school, but as we will see, his method of la canne survived in British Jujutsu.

Tani (called 'The Pocket Hercules' on stage) and Uyenishi (billed as 'Raku' 'the Ju Jitsu Champion of the World'), under the more effective promotion of Scottish strongman and promoter William Bankier, dominated the music hall scene, beating all comers, and it wasn't long before they were joined by other Japanese Jujutsuka such as Taro Miyake, Akitaro Ono, and Mitsuyo Maeda amongst others. Jujutsu was a sensation. William Bankier was a showman and knew how to effectively market and manage Tani and Uyenishi. Bankier was born in Banffshire in Scotland in 1870 and had run away from home to join the circus. This adventure had taken him to Canada and the US before arriving back in London where he appeared on stage under the name 'Apollo'. The public marvelled at how someone as small as Tani could defeat much bigger fighters. On the music hall circuit Tani would have up to 20 opponents a week, often notable Catch wrestlers (although Tani also fought boxers). The rules were those of early Jujutsu contests. He had to submit his opponent. His only condition was that his opponents had to wear a jacket. Tani challenged anyone to a contest, and offered £100 to anyone who could beat him or £20 if they lasted 10 minutes. Tani was thought to be invincible. However, on 24th December 1904 Tani was defeated in little over 5 minutes by fellow Japanese Jujutsuka Taro Miyake, who had also been a student of Mataemon Tanabe and Yotaro Handa. For Tani to fight so prolifically over a period of years and to be so rarely beaten is truly remarkable, even more so given his small stature, standing only 5 feet 3 inches tall. Tani even challenged the world heavyweight wrestling champion George Hackenschmidt, a formidable Russian-born fighter, but the match never came off. Shortly after the loss to Miyake, Tani parted company with Bankier. Tani made a fortune on the music hall scene, but due to gambling lost much of it, which later in his life was probably the reason for a comeback to the music hall scene at the age of 42.

In 1904 Tani and Miyake opened the Japanese School of Jujutsu at 305 Oxford Street W, London, which lasted for just over 2 years. Francis James Norman (1855 – 1926) was a scholar of Japanese martial arts who had lived in

Japan for a period (1888 – 1902), and was commissioned by Tani and Miyake to write a book promoting Jujutsu.

Yukio Tani (seated) and Sadakazu Uyenishi at the Bartitsu club
[With permission from the Bartitsu Society]

In 1905 Norman wrote *The Fighting Man of Japan*, which contained an advert for Tani and Miyake's Japanese School of Jujutsu. This notice advertises classes from 9am to 10pm, and lists a Mr Eida and Mr Kanaya as instructors in addition to Tani and Miyake as chief instructors. In 1906 Tani and Miyake published their own book called *The Game of Ju Jitsu*. The history above suggests Tani was an exceptional Jujutsuka; however, it is interesting to note opinions of the time. For example, Tani/Uyenishi student Percy Longhurst remarked that Tani's success on the music hall scene was largely due to the rules stacking the odds squarely in his favour. Tani's one time colleague Miyake wrote in a letter to *Health and Strength* magazine in 1909 that there were thousands in Japan who could defeat Tani, and even Ernest Harrison wrote that Tani would have no special status in Japan. Regardless of this Tani is rightly an iconic figure in British Judo (see below), and should also be considered so in British Jujutsu for capturing the imagination of the British public and embedding Jujutsu in the national consciousness, which would inspire future generations. Indeed, such was his fame and popularity Tani even starred in a movie called *Ju Jitsu to the Rescue* which was being shown in 1913.

When the Bartitsu School closed in 1902 Sadakazu Uyenishi taught for a brief period at Pierre Vigny's School. In 1903 Uyenishi established his own dojo called the School of Japanese Self Defence, at 31 Golden Square, Piccadilly Circus, in London, bringing former Bartitsu students William and Edith Garrud with him. It is here that British Jujutsu as a style really began to take shape. In 1905 Uyenishi published *The Text Book of Ju-Jutsu as Practised in Japan*. This book would later serve as a foundation for British Jujutsu. At the front of the book Uyenishi wrote a dedication to his father: *'To my father KICHIBE UYENISHI to whose inspiration and example I owe all such success as I may have achieved in life.'* Also listed in the book are Uyenishi's associations, which included being the former instructor to: Riku-gun yo-nan gako (The Military College for Officers); Tai-iku-kai (The Imperial Military College of Physical Training), Shi-han-gako (The School of Instructors), Jun sa kio-shun sho (The Police Training School), All Government Schools in Osaka, and to The Army Gymnastic Staff Head Quarters Gymnasium in Aldershot.

Uyenishi was recognised as an exceptional Jujutsuka and teacher. In a tribute at the end of the 7th edition of Uyenishi's text book, former student Percy Longhurst stated *'Uyenishi's talent as an instructor was equal to his skill as an exponent'*. Longurst further states *'A sportsman according to the best western standards, a gentleman, an artist in his own way, this bespectacled young Japanese, whose refined appearance carried no suggestion of his astonishing physical qualities and powers, a muscular development of all-over excellence that was a delight to the eye, made friends wherever he went'*. Longurst also made note of Uyenishi's physical attributes, stating his height as 5 feet 5 inches, and weight as 9st 2lb. Longhurst made special mention of the strength of Uyenishi's neck. Indeed such was the strength of Uyenishi's neck Longhurst remarked 12 people could hold a pole against his neck and Uyenishi would still escape. Such an exhibition was reported in *Sandow's Magazine* (43:18, January 1902, p28-31), and recorded in the *Electronic Journal of Martial Arts and Sciences* by Joseph Svinth: *'An interesting item in the performance of the Japs was the demonstration of what can be done in the way of strengthening the neck against possible attempts at strangling and garrotting. A Jap was laid full length upon his back, his head resting on the mats. Across his neck a long ash-pole was laid, and upon the ends of this - two on each side - four of the heaviest men were invited to exert the utmost pressure of which they were capable. The pole was, of course, pliant, but that notwithstanding, the feat was an extraordinary one; rendered not the less so by the clever way in which the Jap wriggled himself free from the pole, while the latter was still under the heavy pressure of the four strangers. The performance concluded with a brief wrestling bout - curtailed in view of the promised match between Uyenishi and the Cornish and Devonshire Professional*

Heavyweight Champion, which we were destined not to see - between the pair, one lying on his back and protecting himself from attack with his feet. This was an exceptionally clever exhibition, the recumbent man resembling nothing so much, in his methods, as a fighting owl at bay. All efforts of his opponent to rush in were foiled, the climax being reached when the prostate combatant administered a neat coup de grâce with his feet that jerked the other's legs from under him and brought him to the mats with a sounding thwack upon his back. How far the contest could be considered a serious one it is impossible to say, but the effect was good.'

In an article titled 'Exhibitions and Challenges' by the Bartitsu historian Tony Wolf in 2006, an excerpt of Armand Cherpillod's 1933 autobiography revealed another of Uyenishi's early challenges against Klemsky, a Russian wrestler and strongman:

'The theatre was completely filled by a public intrigued by the innovation of this fight and drawn by the reputation of the Russian wrestler. As soon as Klemsky had donned the Japanese jacket, the two men came to grips. Both had been caught by their jackets, and in less time than one could take to tell it, Uyenishi had whirled his powerful adversary into the air and had let him fall down on his back.

As quick as a flash, the Japanese leaped onto the Russian and seized him by the collar of the jacket, on hand on each side of his neck, by crossing the wrists, and learnedly exerted the famous pressure on the carotid arteries which brings choking, and even unconsciousness. The hold did not seem to have any effect on the Russian who simply smiled at the audience. Astonished by this resistance, the Japanese wrestler's eyes gleamed with malice.

He rolled across the ground past the Russian while preserving his hold and, to increase the force of the pressure on the neck, planted his two feet in the pit of Klemsky's stomach. This tightened the grip so extremely that a net of blood escaped from the mouth of Klemsky and sprinkled his face. It was only then that Uyenishi released his hold and let fall beside him the apparently lifeless body of the Russian.

The public believed that Klemsky had died. They howled their anger and their disapproval of Uyenishi. This latter, triumphant, appeared to be insensitive to the hostile remonstrations of the public. He went to sit down on the sidelines, beside his compatriot, in the manner of the tailors at work, by crossing his legs beneath him. And while the spectators redoubled their cries, our two Japanese entered into an animated conversation and even laughed together, contemplating the victim who did not give any sign of life.

Suddenly, one of them rose, as if driven by a spring, and approached Klemsky. He leaned on the body of the Russian and gave some sort of vibration or massage to the cardiac area, which revived the victim gradually. Then, to the great astonishment of the audience who were now gasping, Klemsky opened his eyes and asked where he was. This seemed magical, and even more than before, Jiu-jitsu appeared to be a most mysterious form of fighting. When someone asked Klemsky for his impression of the event, he said that while losing consciousness he had heard the sound of bells. The spectacle was over. Nobody other than

Klemsky wanted to risk a voyage in the Nirvana, even for one very short moment. The fact remained that on this evening, Jiu-jitsu had acquired great respect throughout England.'

Thanks to the research of Tony Wolf we know now that the Russian also went by the name of John Clempert, a wrestler and escape artist who was frequently billed as 'The man they cannot hang' on account of his neck strength.

In 1907 Uyenishi travelled to Spain with Miyake and Maeda, leaving his dojo in the hands of his senior student William Garrud. Uyenishi would perform demonstrations offering 500 pesetas to anyone who could defeat him in a wrestling (Jujutsu) contest. Whilst touring with Miyake and Maeda in Spain it was noted that the Japanese would whisper instructions to each other while competing. Uyenishi gave demonstrations in Barcelona, Madrid, Santander, Bilbao, Valladilid, Toulouse, San Sebastian, Zaragoza, Logrono, Valencia, and Alicante with the Circus Parma. Uyenishi would also travel to Portugal and perform in Lisbon. In addition to challenge matches he also performed demonstrations of strength with people pushing bamboo canes against his throat as above. In 1909 Uyenishi opened a dojo in Madrid. In mid-1910 there was an accident in which there was a fight amongst Uyenishi's students. It is not known what happened but it caused Uyenishi to return to Osaka, where he died some time after. Although Uyenishi was only present in the UK for a relatively short time, he would leave behind a considerable legacy.

Another Jujutsu club at the time was the Anglo-Japanese Institute of Self Defence at 3 Vernon Place, Bloomsbury Square, London, which was run by Vernon Smith and where Uyenishi amongst others was employed as an instructor. By this time there were more Japanese living in London who may also have been taking advantage of the Jujutsu craze to earn some money.

It is also important to reflect at this point that traditional Koryu Jujutsu does not generally have a sporting nature. However, we know that there were many Jujutsu contests towards the end of the Edo period in Japan as mentioned above, and Tani, Uyenishi, and others actively participated in contests on their arrival in England. Thus, from its beginnings, British Jujutsu has been competitive.

Portrait of Sadakazu Uyenishi from William Garrud's book The Complete Jujitsuan [Public doman, 1914]

Gunji Koizumi Arrives

In May 1906 Gunji Koizumi arrived, with only sixpence to his name, in North Wales aboard the *SS Romford* and found employment as chief instructor of the Kara Ashikaga School of Jujutsu in Liverpool, which had advertised teaching Jujutsu '*as taught in the Yoshimosa School in Japan.*'

It would seem now however that the instructor Kara Ashikaga was fictional, as was the Yoshimosa School, and the Kara Ashikaga School subsequently turned out to have been a correspondence school run by a Mr Thomas without a dojo.

Nevertheless, Koizumi tried to make a success of the Kara Ashikaga for two months before 'Mr Thomas' decided that it was not financially viable. During his brief stay in Liverpool Koizumi met Judoka 4th dan Akitaro Ono, who was performing at the Olympia music hall. Ono must have told Koizumi of the Jujutsu in London, as in August 1906 Koizumi headed south. However, before Koizumi left the Kara Ashikaga, Mr Thomas, perhaps wanting to test his new instructor, found a wrestler for Koizumi to fight. The story told by Richard Bowen (*100 Years of Judo in Great Britain, Volume 1*) reports that Koizumi had warned the wrestler not to hold on, a warning which was duly ignored. Koizumi threw the wrestler with a shoulder throw and landed on the wrestler, causing him to stop breathing. Koizumi then had to revive the wrestler using Katsu (resuscitation).

The Bartitsu historian Tony Wolf discovered that the correspondence course offered by the Kara Ashikaga seems to have been based on Harry Hall Skinner's 1904 book *Jiu-Jitsu: A Comprehensive and Copiously Illustrated Treatise on the Wonderful Japanese Method of Attack and Self Defense*. Although Skinner is credited as the author, Wolf noted that it is possibly more likely that the book was actually developed by B.H. Kuwashima, who demonstrated all the moves in the book and who was the Jujutsu instructor at Columbia University in New York.

It is not known what Koizumi, a true Jujutsu expert, made of the Kara Ashikaga when he arrived in Liverpool, but we do know that Koizumi rapidly made his way to London, where he trained in the dojo of Uyenishi (and the Garruds), and taught at the Royal Naval Volunteers, and Regent Street Polytechnic, until he departed for the USA in 1907. It was during this period in London that Koizumi came into contact with Mitsuyo Maeda, who had been a student of Tsunejiro Tomita, one of Kano's first senior grades in Kodokan Judo. Akitaro Ono, another Judoka, also trained at this time. Their influence is important as they first introduced Koizumi to Kodokan Judo. Koizumi's previous experience had been in Jujutsu with firstly Tago Nobushige of Tenjin Shinyo Ryu, and subsequently Yamada Nobukatsu of Shin Shin Ryu, and Tsunejiro Akishima of Akishima Ryu.

The Kara Ashikaga was not the only effort from the era to try and profit on the fame of Jujutsu. Another notable individual to profit from Jujutsu was Captain Sydney Temple Leopold McLaglen (1884-1951), known as Leopold McLaglen.

McLaglen certainly looked every bit the action hero and claimed to have learned Jujutsu from childhood from a Japanese family servant. By 1908 he was making the highly dubious claim to have won the 'Jiujitsu Championship of the World'. The article by Bartitsu historian Tony Wolf 'The Martial Shenanigans of Leopold McLaglen' states that McLaglen's claim to be a world champion came from his questionable defeat of a Japanese fighter in 1907. Wolf quoted the comments of a local reporter present at the fight: *'For two hours the spectators saw nothing but Kanada crouching on the mat with McLaglen on top of him and there was little, if any, jiu-jitsu to the performance. It was apparent to everyone that McLaglen's knowledge of the game could be covered with a pinhead.'*

In 1913 Leopold McLaglen travelled to South Africa to tour music halls. Here he met a well-known South African wrestler called Tromp Van Diggellen. Together they would perform shows where 'Leopold the Great' would demonstrate his Jujutsu skills against Van Diggellen. Knowing McLaglen to be of limited skill Van Diggellen went along with the charade, putting on a show. On one occasion McLaglen grew overconfident and challenged anyone in the audience. Unfortunately for him the challenge was met by a young boxer called Robbie Roberts who gave him a terrible beating! Despite clearly lacking any real Jujitsu knowledge McLaglen went on to become a Jujutsu instructor to soldiers and police in what was a very colourful and controversial life.

It is a little known fact that Mitsuyo Maeda (1878 – 1941) spent time in London. Maeda is much better known for pioneering Judo in Brazil, where he arrived in 1914. Maeda was born in Hirosaki City (formerly known as Funasawa), and growing up he learnt sumo from his father. While at school in Tokyo he learnt Tenjin Shinyo Ryu, before studying Kodokan Judo. Maeda left Japan for the US in 1904, where he toured, giving Jujutsu/Judo demonstrations with Tsunejiro Tomita before travelling to Cuba, where he defeated Adobamond, considered the best Cuban fighter. On February 8, 1907, Maeda arrived in England. During his brief stay in the UK it appears Maeda also gave demonstrations in Scotland, including in September 1908 at the Northern Games in Inverness. Maeda would then tour Europe before returning to South America, arriving in Brazil in 1914. Maeda gave demonstration matches, now under the stage name of 'Conde Koma', before embarking on another tour of Europe and then returning to Brazil in 1917. Maeda was an incredible fighter, winning over 2000 fights in his professional career, which led to him being called 'the toughest man who ever lived'. In 1917, a 14-year-old Carlos Gracie and Luiz França became students of Maeda and became great exponents of the art. Carlos Gracie, along with his younger brother Hélio, subsequently founded Gracie Jiu Jitsu, which aided the development of Brazilian Jiu Jitsu. Incidentally, Carlos and Hélio Gracie were 4th generation British immigrants – their great-grandfather George Gracie had arrived from Scotland in 1826. Maeda stayed in Brazil for the rest of his life. The Kodokan promoted Maeda to 6th dan in 1929. On the 27th of November, 1941, the day before Maeda died of kidney disease, the Kodokan promoted him to 7th dan.

Another student of Uyenishi was William E. Steers, who travelled to Japan to study Jujutsu with Ernest Harrison and returned to Uyenishi's dojo in 1904. In 1912 Steers travelled back to Japan and studied Kodokan Judo with Jigoro Kano.

Other notable students of Tani and Uyenishi at the time were wrestling friends such as Percy Longhurst, W Bruce Sutherland, and Percy Bickerdike.

Another Jujutsu club in the UK in this period was at the University of Cambridge. This dojo was part of Trinity College and was opened in 1906 by a Mr. Evelyn Charles Donaldson Rawlins. This was a private dojo but did receive periodic instruction from the likes of Tani and Koizumi. Today the University of Cambridge club is regarded to be the oldest Judo/Jujutsu club in the country.

Before Uyenishi left the UK it is worth noting his influence on another individual of note. Born in 1857, Robert Stephenson Smyth Baden-Powell (later Lord Baden-Powell) led a distinguished military career, mainly in Africa, achieving the rank of Lieutenant-General. On returning to England in 1903 Baden-Powell discovered that a military training manual he had authored, *Aids to Scouting*, had become very popular with youth organisations, which prompted him to write a revised edition specifically for youths. Baden-Powell witnessed a demonstration of Jujutsu by Uyenishi at Windsor Castle in 1906 at which he was greatly impressed. In 1907 Baden-Powell held a scout camp at Brownsea Island which was considered the start of the scouting movement, at which Jujutsu was demonstrated. In the first set of scout merit badges produced there was a 'Master at Arms' in which the scout was required to have participated in one of a number of combat activities, one of which was Jujutsu.

THE SUFFRAGETTE THAT KNEW JIU-JITSU.

Cartoon depicting 'The Suffragette that knew Jiu-Jitsu'

Suffrajutsu

It is important to note that the practice of Jujutsu in London at the beginning of the 20th century was not exclusively male. By 1903 women such as Phoebe Roberts and Emily Watts were training and teaching Jujutsu at Uyenishi's Golden Square dojo. Later Phoebe Roberts would teach women's classes at Tani and Miyake's Oxford Street dojo, and it is here where she met future husband Hirano Juso. Emily Watts published the book *The Fine Art of Jujutsu* in 1906 demonstrating Jujutsu techniques. However, perhaps the most important female Jujutsu practitioner and teacher of the time was Edith Garrud.

Edith Garrud demonstrating a wrist throw (kote gaeshi)
[Permission from the Bartitsu Society].

Edith and her husband William Garrud were first introduced to Jujutsu by Edward William Barton-Wright at his Bartitsu club in 1899. Both William and Edith would subsequently become students of Sadakuza Uyenishi at his Golden Square dojo in 1903. When Uyenishi left the UK the running of the club fell to William Garrud, with Edith teaching women's and children's classes.

The start of the 20th century was a time of great inequality and women were not able to vote. Movements were mobilised to take direct action against this inequality, and one such movement was the Women's Social and Political Union (WSPU), founded in 1903 by Emmeline Pankhurst; this movement became known as the suffragettes. The suffragettes campaigned for equality, but during demonstrations some claimed to have been beaten and sexually assaulted by police and male vigilantes. In order to combat this, members of the WSPU turned to Jujutsu. By 1910 Edith Garrud was teaching Jujutsu in suffragette-only classes and the term 'Suffrajitsu' was in common usage. According to Richard Bowen (*100 Years of Judo in Great Britain, Volume 1*), Edith and William Garrud separated sometime in 1910. William wanted a divorce but Edith refused on the grounds that her name was so famous she didn't want another woman to use it!

In 1913 the government passed the so-called 'Cat and Mouse Act' which allowed hunger-striking suffragette prisoners to be released and then re-arrested once their health had recovered. To prevent the re-arrest of activists the WSPU formed the Bodyguard – a 30 strong group that undertook 'dangerous activities'. Edith Garrud trained the Bodyguard in Jujutsu and in the use of Indian clubs which they would carry hidden in their dresses. To avoid the attention of the police the lessons for the Bodyguard took place in a series of secret locations. At the outbreak of World War I (WWI) the suffragette movement was suspended and the Bodyguard disbanded. Following WWI some women (over 30 and appropriately qualified) got the vote after the Representation of the People Act 1918, and finally, in 1928, women gained electoral equality with men with the Representation of the People (Equal Franchise) Act 1928. The Garruds continued to teach Jujutsu up until 1925 when they sold their dojo. Edith spent the rest of her life engaged in various charitable activities until her death in 1971 at the age of 99.

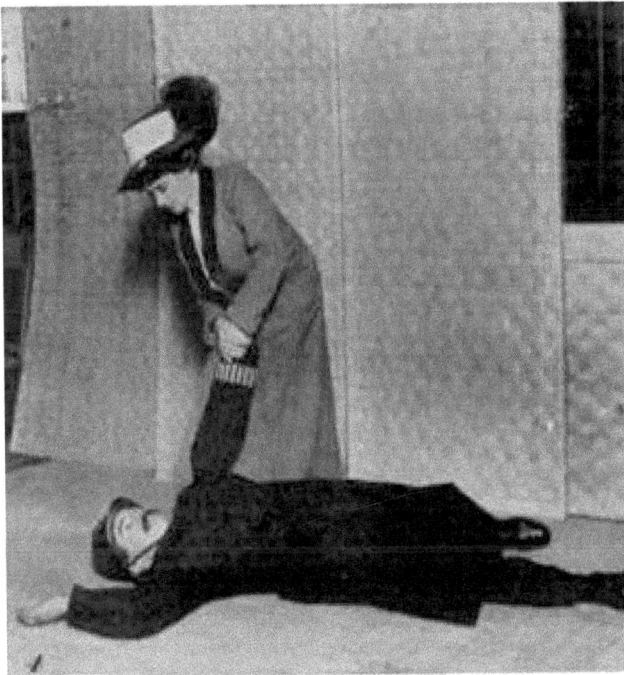

Jujutsu and the Budokwai

The Jujutsu clubs of Tani on Oxford Street and Uyenishi's Golden Square dojo were being supported by William Bankier's Health and Strength League. Uyenishi left the UK, handing the reins of his dojo to William Garrud, in 1906. By 1910 Koizumi had returned from the USA. In the time since the first Japanese Jujutsuka had arrived in London they had apparently awarded black sashes (rather than black belts) to many of their students, potentially including Jack Britten, who started training in 1910. William E. Steers set sail for Japan in 1903 where he learnt Tenjin Shinyo Ryu from Ernest Harrison. Upon his return to London Steers trained with Uyenishi, where he met Koizumi in 1906. Steers would travel to Tokyo in 1912 to train with Kano at the Kodokan, where he became one of the first Westerners (after Harrison) to obtain the rank of Shodan (1st dan black belt), and at the age of 55. It is said that when he returned to London he demonstrated an 'evangelical zeal' for practising Judo.

In 1918 Koizumi, now aged 32, used his own money to lease 15 Lower Grosvenor Place, London. The dojo was called the Budokwai and was initially for the practice of Japanese martial arts in general. The Budokwai opened its doors on the 26th January 1918 with Yukio Tani as its first chief instructor. Amongst the early members of the Budokwai were William Steers and Ernest Harrison, now back in the UK, who exerted a strong Kodokan Judo influence. On May 31, 1919, the Budokwai hosted an exhibition by Sonobe Masatada, the grandmaster of Jikishin Kage Ryu, which included Kendo, Nabebutajutsu (the use of pan lids as bucklers), Nitojutsu (fencing with a sword in each hand), Kusarigamajutsu (the use of the chain and sickle), as well as Jujutsu. Female master Hino Yoshiko also demonstrated Naginatajutsu (halberd or pole mounted axe).

Later, British Jujutsuka Terry Wingrove (see below) trained with Sonobe's successor, the female Soke Sonobe Hideo, in Japan in the 1960s, and described her to me as: 'the deadliest thing on two legs.'

In 1920 Jigoro Kano was visiting the Olympic Games in Antwerp as a member of the International Olympic Committee when Steers arranged for him to visit the Budokwai. At midnight on the 15th of July 1920 Steers and Koizumi met Kano at Waterloo Station. With Kano was Kodokan 4th dan Hikochi Aida who Kano had selected to be a Judo teacher at the Budokwai. Kano used this visit to the UK to affiliate as much Jujutsu as possible into the Kodokan. In the December of 1920 Kano promoted Koizumi and Tani to Nidans (2nd dan black belts) at the Budokwai; neither Koizumi nor Tani had practised Judo previously. The Budokwai had converted to Kodokan Judo.

The Budokwai continued promoting Judo and recruiting affiliated clubs. In response to the Budokwai converting to Judo William Bankier's Health and Strength League may have founded the British Ju Jitsu Society (BJJS) in 1924 with Percy Bickerdike as the first secretary, and along with other enthusiasts of the time including Percy Longhurst and W Bruce Sutherland. However, it is known that William Bankier became a member of the Budokwai in 1927. According to James Shortt in *Beginning Jiu Jitsu: Ryoi Shinto Style*, because the British Ju Jitsu Society would not become Budokwai affiliates, the Budokwai refused to recognise them. It is unclear how successful the BJJS were, with the British Newspaper Archive containing a limited amount of references between 1928 and 1932. Richard Bowen, in *100 Years of Judo in Great Britain, Volume 2*, does however make reference to the BJJS.

Harry H. Hunter had returned from Japan calling himself the 'Jujitsu Champion of Europe'. In an interview for the *Liverpool Echo*, March 1st 1924, at Hercules Athletic Club, Lord Street, Liverpool, Hunter discussed the virtues of his 'Super Jujitsu' system and threw out a challenge to anyone, including the heavyweight boxing champion of the world! In this article Hunter stated his weight as 10 stone and 10 pounds. Hunter issued a similar challenge in the *Liverpool Echo* of 15th July, 1925, and on 7th October 1925 was advertising a Jujutsu versus boxing contest.

Hunter's challenges did not go unnoticed by the Jujutsu/wrestling community either. Richard Bowen cites an unknown newspaper article from 1926 where an Alfred J. Morgan had challenged Hunter to a contest, even offering to come to Hunter's dojo in Liverpool. Alf Morgan had some pedigree as an amateur catch wrestler, and according to Richard Morris (see below) had been a student of Yukio Tani (not noted by Bowen). Morgan stated his weight as 9 stone and 9 pounds and his age as 40. Morgan defeated Hunter and *The Ju-Jitsuan*, the monthly publication of the BJJS, wrote to Morgan on the 31st August 1926 to congratulate him on becoming the 'European Jujitsu Champion' and asking him to become involved in the BJJS. This letter was signed by a G Williams of Coventry who is listed as a Founder of the BJJA on the letterhead along with A.W.M. Hayward and C. F. Gibbs. Bowen also records that the BJJS issued a certificate stating that Morgan was a 'Master of the British Jujitsu Society'. We will mention Alf Morgan again in a later chapter.

Morgan and Hunter were in fact due to have a rematch, but Hunter pulled out and a Jim Hipkiss stepped in and on the 16th March 1927 defeated Morgan in London for the Great British Jujitsu Championship. Hipkiss was also a wrestling champion and defended his titles for more than a decade, defeating Morgan a further two times in 1928 and in 1934. Hipkiss joined the Budokwai in 1929 but would last only two years. The Budokwai didn't approve of fighting for money and so Hipkiss tendered his resignation, which was duly accepted. Hipkiss was however largely responsible for establishing Judo/Jujitsu in Birmingham and in the Midlands. During WWII Hipkiss was in the Home Guard and became well known for his 1941 publication *Unarmed Combat*, which was a training manual for the Home Guard.

Further insight into the BJJS comes from recently uncovered documents. On the 22nd March 2018 a member of the public came across several old Jujitsu documents when going through her grandparents' artefacts and sent them to BJJA(GB) Chairman Martin Dixon, who subsequently discussed them with BJJA(GB) historian David Brough, who discussed them with me.

Jim Hipkiss performing Kani Basami (scissors throw) on Alf Morgan at the British Jujitsu School on Church Street, Birmingham, in December 1928.
[Picture provided by Tony Underwood, BJC]

Based on comparisons with related correspondence it would appear that the documents date from the late 1920s/early 1930s. The documents include a letter of invitation to join the BJJS signed by G Williams, a membership form, a booklet called *The Art of Ju-jitsu* by G Williams, and a prospectus. The prospectus has some particularly interesting insights. For example, the prospectus quotes: *'We have many testimonials from satisfied members and from famous Ju-jitsu champions such as Hipkiss, Morgan, Gotz, Butcher, McCarthy, Saddington, etc etc who say "Other lessons are not a patch on yours".'* The prospectus also provides information on a correspondence course and postal examinations offering three levels: Graduate of the BJJS – upon passing the Preliminary Diploma Examination; Fellow of the BJJS – upon passing the Intermediate Diploma Examination; Master of the BJJS – upon passing the Final Diploma Examination. Furthermore, upon becoming a member you would receive the badge of the BJJS and learn *'the secret sign of the Society'*. Within the prospectus the badge was described as: *'The badge is artistically enamelled in dark blue round the outer circle and a light blue centre. The symbolic figure and the wording stand out in gilt. The design altogether is very pleasing and appropriate.'*

BJJA(GB) historian David Brough came across the BJJS badge being sold as a lapel pin on eBay in Canada. From the maker's stamp (W Miller 118 Branston

St Birmingham) we know the badge was manufactured before 1928. How did the badge end up in Canada? We know that Harry H Hunter left Liverpool for Canada in 1929, where he remained until his death in 1941 age 57. Pure speculation, but it is tantalising to speculate that this pin badge could have belonged to Harry H Hunter. Further, we may speculate that the symbol on the badge is indeed the secret sign of the society. The use of the term 'Master' is also interesting as we know several British Jujutsuka would recognise a 'Master' level (e.g. Jack Britten). Does this suggest an involvement with the BJJS?

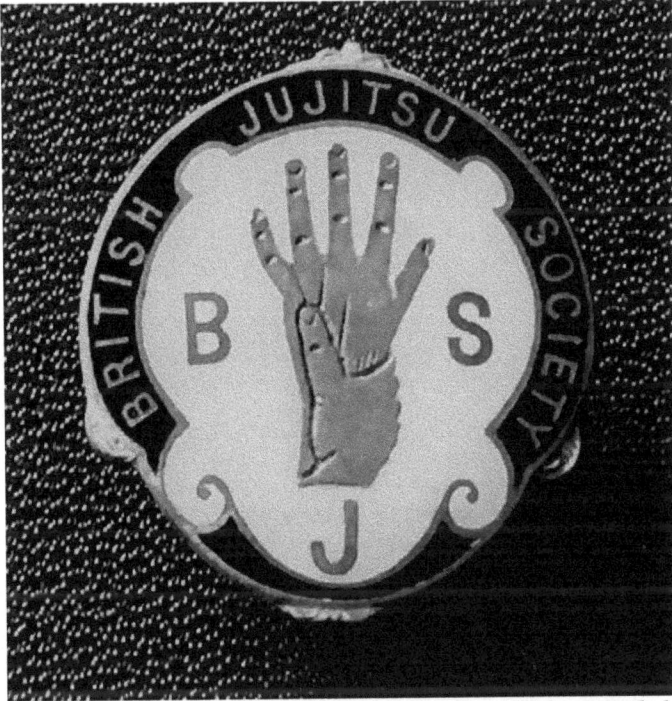

Pin badge of the BJJS badge manufactured in 1928. Did this once belong to Hunter? [Picture provided by David Brough]

We also know that many of the books on Jujitsu published at this time were from members of the BJJS. In 1914 William Garrud published *The Complete Jujitsuan* and indeed members of the BJJS referred to each other as Jujitsuans, which was also the name of the BJJS periodical. Percy Longhurst was a former student of Uyenishi, a member of the BJJS, and was a prolific author on the subject of Jujutsu including his 1923 book *Ju-jutsu & Judo*. W Bruce Sutherland took up Jujitsu after losing a contest to Tani in 1905. Sutherland ran a Physical Culture school in Edinburgh and taught Jujitsu to the army, the police, and to the Boy Scouts. Sutherland published *Ju-Jitsu: Self-Defence* circa 1920. Born in Edinburgh in 1879, Sutherland would father nine children with his wife Agnes, and held the world record for the longest continual played game of golf!

Percy Longhurst was also an advocate of Pierre Vigny's method of la canne and it is featured in Longhurst's book of 1906 *Jiu Jitsu and Other Methods of Self Defence*. One of Vigny's la canne students at the Bartitsu club was Percy Rolt, who subsequently taught Henry G. Lang. In 1923, Lang, an officer of the Indian Police, wrote the now classic training book *The "Walking Stick" Method of Self Defence*, which was based on Vigny's la canne. Lang's book was translated into Hebrew in 1941 and became the basis for self-defence training of up to 50,000 Jews living in Palestine.

JU-JUTSU & JUDO

BY
PERCY LONGHURST

6^D NET

9

WARNE'S "RECREATION" BOOK

Jujutsu books published by members of the BJJS. Top panel is the cover of a 1st edition of Percy Longhursts 1923 book Ju-jutsu & Judo. The other is the cover of W Bruce Sutherlands Ju-jitsu Self-Defence c.1920

War Shapes Jujutsu

WWII saw another strand of Jujutsu introduced to the UK. Men in the armed forces were taught combatives, or hand-to-hand fighting techniques. The system of combatives taught to allied servicemen during WWII was one developed by William Ewart Fairbairn.

Fairbairn was born in 1885 and started his career in the military with the Royal Marines in 1901 when he served in Korea. In 1907 he joined the Shanghai Municipal Police (SMP). The SMP policed the Shanghai International Settlement. At the time Shanghai was an open port leased by the Chinese to others for trade and consisted of the International Settlement, the French Concession, and the Chinese Territory. It was considered one of the most dangerous port cities in the world, over-run with organised crime gangs, nationalist and separatist groups, drug dealers, and any other type of criminal you can think of. Being in the SMP was not for the faint hearted and required fighting skills and ability.

As noted by Richard Bowen (*100 Years of Judo in Great Britain, Volume 2*), early in his career in the SMP Fairbairn was subject to a sustained attack while on patrol which put him in hospital. Awaking in hospital Fairbairn found a card on his bedside table that read 'Professor Okada Jujutsu and Bonesetting.' Fairbairn would spend three and a half years with Okada learning Shin no Shinto Ryu Jujutsu. Fairbairn would also learn Kodokan Judo, for which he earned a 1st dan in 1926 and a 2nd dan in 1931. Fairbairn also learnt Chinese martial arts including Ch'uan Fa from Tsai Ching Tung (thought to be the Yin style Bagua master Cui Zhendong who moved to Shanghai). In the SMP Fairbairn was allegedly involved in over 600 non-training street fights where he honed his fighting skills, leading him to develop his own system of unarmed combat called 'Defendu'. Fairbairn's system was developed on his fighting experience, of which he had plenty, and he was covered in scars from head to toe to prove it.

During WWII Fairbairn and his colleague from the SMP Eric Anthony Sykes were commissioned into the British Army as officers to teach allied forces combatives. Initially this was part of the Special Operations Executive (SOE); Fairbairn and Sykes would teach commandos at the training centre in Lochailort on the west coast of Scotland from 1940 - 1942. In 1942 Fairbairn went to teach at Camp X on the shores of Lake Ontario, Canada, where he taught combatives to the Coordinator of Information (COI), which would become the Office of Strategic Services (OSS), and ultimately the Central Intelligence Agency (CIA). Fairbairn taught what he called 'gutter fighting': winning at all costs. In his 1943 publication *Get Tough! How to win in hand to hand fighting (as taught to the British Commandos)* Fairbairn states: *'The methods described in this book I have carefully worked out and developed over a period of many years. They owe something to the famous Japanese judo (jiu-jutso), and something else to Chinese boxing. But, largely, they were developed from my own experience and observation of how most effectively to deal with the ruffians, thugs, bandits, and bullies of one of the roughest water-front areas in the world.'* Fairbairn died in 1960 aged 75 at his home in West Sussex.

Koizumi and Tani remained in the UK during WWII, and in fact during WWII Koizumi and colleagues ran a volunteer ambulance service to help the people of London during the German bombardments. After the war, in 1948, Koizumi helped establish the British Judo Association (BJA), and a few days afterwards the European Judo Union (EJU). The EJU was subsequently dissolved so the International Judo Federation (IJF) could be established. It was decided that the IJF headquarters would be the Kodokan in Tokyo and so an EJU was reconstituted along with other regional administrative centres. Ernest Harrison was also still practising Judo at the Budokwai. Harrison was awarded his 4th dan in Judo from Koizumi in 1956, aged 82. Harrison died in 1961 aged 87. On the 15th of April 1965, Koizumi, aged 79, committed suicide after feeling he had contributed as much as he could to humanity. Despite suffering a stroke in 1937 Yukio Tani continued to help from the sidelines at the Budokwai until his death on 24th of January 1950 aged 68.

Of the many great Judoka to graduate through the Budokwai another worthy of mention is Tani's student Trevor Pryce Leggett. Leggett was born in 1914 and started training at the Budokwai in 1932 under Yukio Tani, grading to 3rd dan. In 1938 Leggett travelled to Japan, where he was also stationed during WWII at the British embassy. Leggett would achieve his 4-6th dan gradings at the Kodokan. Leggett would write many books, not just about Judo, but on Japanese culture and other subjects, and in 1984 was awarded the 'Order of the Sacred Treasure' by the Japanese government for his services in introducing Japanese culture to the UK. Leggett died in London after suffering a stroke in 2000.

The BJA would not however remain the only governing body for Judo. Pat Butler had joined the Budowkai in 1947 and had become its publicity manager. In 1955 Butler left the BJA and established the Amateur Judo Association (AJA) with fellow Judoka Harry Ewen. The AJA would grow to become a very large organisation with many talented Judoka, but it is worth mentioning two names now who would become relevant to British Jujutsu in the future: in the mid-1960s the North West Area secretary for the AJA was Frank Garner, and the national coach was Norman Grundy. Another Judo organisation formed in 1958 was the British Judo Council (BJC). This was formed by Japanese Judoka Kenshiro Abbe (see below) and Masutaro Otani.

At the end of WWII in 1945 the US occupation government in Japan issued a directive for the dissolution of military related organisations, leading the Dai Nippon Butoku Kai (DNBK) to voluntarily cease operating. The DNBK would reopen in 1953, with a new charter, driven by Kumao Ohno, who made the DNBK once again a presence in Japanese martial arts. His Excellency, Jigo Higashifushimi, the supreme abbot of Shorenin Temple in Kyoto, a brother to the late Empress Kotaigo of Emperor Hirohito, became chairman of the new DNBK and was later recognised as its Sosai.

After the war in Japan another martial arts organisation of importance to British Jujutsu was formed. In 1951, a group of prominent Japanese martial artists got together to discuss the first open demonstration of martial arts in Japan since the end of WWII. A result of this meeting was the formation of the National Japan Health Association. It would later be called the Kokusai Budoin, International Martial Arts Federation (IMAF), and was initially founded by Kyuzo Mifune, Kazuo Ito and Shizuya Sato of Judo; Hakudo Nakayama and Hiromasa Takano of Kendo; Hironori Ohtsuka of Karate-do; and Kiyotaka Wake and Sueo Kiyoura. Following the first IMAF demonstration in 1952, members of IMAF continued to promote the practice of Japanese martial arts throughout Japan and ultimately would expand to promote Japanese martial arts around the world, including in the UK. In terms of the type of organisation Kokusai Budoin is, it can be considered very similar to the DNBK described above.

Hironori Ohtsuka was born on June 1 1892 in Shimodate City, Ibaragi, Japan. He was the first son of Dr. Tokujuro Ohtsuka and his first teacher was his great uncle Chojiro Ebashi, a member of the samurai class and Jujutsu teacher of the Shindo Yoshin Ryu. From the age of 13 he studied the art under Shihan Shinzaburo Nakayama Sensei, who was also adept in Jikishin Kage Ryu swordsmanship.

He began attending the famous Waseda University in 1910 and continued his Jujutsu studies. In 1917 Ohtsuka joined the Kawasaki Bank. During the year he met Morihei Ueshiba Sensei, the founder of Aikido, and this began a deep influential friendship.

Shindo Yoshin Ryu was founded by Katsunosuke Matsuoka (1836 – 1898), making it a very young style as Koryu go. Matsuoka originally studied Yoshin Ryu Jujutsu and was also a student of Jikishin Kage Ryu Kenjutsu and Hokushin Ittoryu Kenjutsu as well as being a certified teacher of Tenjin Shinyoryu Jujutsu. It was in 1864 that Matsuoka formed his own style of Yoshin Ryu Jujutsu, calling it Shindo Yoshin Ryu Jujutsu. The next generation was Matakichi Inose (1852 – 1921) and finally Ohtsuka Sensei's teacher Tatsusaburo Nakayama (1870 – 1933). It is sometimes stated that Ohtsuka was the 4th grandmaster of Shindo Yoshin Ryu, but this is probably not the case. Tatsusaburo Nakayama was not the 3rd head-master of Shindo Yoshin Ryu as is frequently stated. In 1917, the 2nd head-master, Motokichi Inose, awarded Tatsuo Matsuoka, grandson of Shindo Yoshin Ryu's founder, a menkyo kaiden and handed over the Sokeship. Tatsuo Matsuoka died without formally appointing a successor.

In 1922 Ohtsuka met the Karate master Gichin Funakoshi. Ohtsuka had become Chief Instructor of Shindo Yoshin Ryu Jujutsu at the age of just 30, and an assistant instructor at Funakoshi Sensei's Karate Dojo. In 1924 the two met Yasuhiro Konishi, who would become the next piece in the Karate puzzle. Konishi was a well respected Kendoka and had studied Muso Ryu Jujutsu at the age of six and then in high school switched to Takenouchi Ryu Jujutsu – he was therefore a natural Karate practitioner.

In the 1920s Ohtsuka also trained with Choki Motobu. It has been suggested Motobu had no respect for Gichin Funakoshi, but it seems he did respect the young Ohtsuka. Motobu taught his version of Naihanchi (Tekki) to Ohtsuka, who may well have reciprocated with Jujutsu teachings. At this time Ohtsuka also had the chance to train with Shito Ryu head Kenwa Mabuni. The book *Nihon Budo Taikei* tells of a meeting at Yasuhiro Konishi's dojo in 1929 between Choki

Motobu and Gichin Funakoshi. Also present were Hironori Ohtsuka and a Judo 4th dan who was accompanying Motobu. Motobu arranged a challenge in which the Judoka took a grip on Funakoshi's collar and sleeve. Motobu then said, "Now you are so proud of your basic kata, show me what value they have in this situation. Do what you wish to escape." It is obvious that the odds were greatly against Funakoshi, the much younger Judoka having established a firm grip. He reportedly tried to disengage with Soto-uke and Uchi-uke with no success and he was lifted up and thrown against the wall of the dojo. Ohtsuka Sensei was then asked to try his luck. He rose to the challenge and because of his Jujutsu background had no difficulty in dealing with the situation.

His desire to adapt Funakoshi Sensei's Karate by introducing more kumite elements caused him to grow apart from his teacher. In 1929 Ohtsuka left Shotokan to form his own style of Wado Ryu with the full blessing of Funakoshi. Ohtsuka admitted in later years that it took him another 10 years before what he wanted was actually formulated into Wado Ryu as we know it today. At this point, in 1929, he had studied Karate for eight years and was around 38 years old.

His approach to Karate and Jujutsu was extremely progressive. In 1934 his son Jiro was born and he also registered his style of Karate as Wado Ryu.

In 1938 aged 46 he was awarded the Renshi title, implying a grade of around 4th or 5th dan. In 1942 Ohtsuka Sensei was awarded the rank of Kyoshi Go, suggesting a grade of at least 6th or 7th dan. In 1963, a three man team left Japan to demonstrate Wado-Ryu Karate to America and Europe. The team was composed of Arakama Sensei, Takashima Sensei and Suzuki Sensei.

Tatsuo Suzuki introduced Wado Ryu Karate to England, although technically it had already been taught here by Hiroo Mochizuki, who began his studies in Yoseikan/Shotokan but then trained with Ohtsuka Sensei. Among the early British pioneers in Wado were Ticky Donovan and John Smith. Other Japanese Wado Ryu instructors of the time were Shiomitsu Sensei and Takamizawa Sensei.

In 1966 Ohtsuka Sensei was awarded Kun Goto Kyokujitsu Shou (something like an OBE) by Emperor Hirohito for his dedication to the introduction and teaching of Karate.

On October 9, 1972, the Kokusai Budoin (International Martial Arts Federation) awarded Ohtsuka the title of Shodai Karate-do Meijin Judan (first-generation Karate master 10th dan); this was the first time this honour had been bestowed on a Karate practitioner.

In *Karate Jutsu* I theorised a link between Yoshin Ryu's Hakuda and Okinawan Karate. Hakuda aspect refers to southwestern Japanese Jujutsu such as taught by Akiyama. This was a percussive art and in many ways was a mainland Japanese version of Karate.

Hironori Ohtsuka wrote about that link: *'Every year, for purposes of promoting the Japanese martial-arts, the Butokuden in Kyoto held a national festival. In 1938, the festival focused on the originators of each martial art, however, no originator of Japanese Karate had been identified. I named the originator of the first true Japanese style of Karate-Do as Shiro-Yoshitoki Akiyama (the founder of Shinto Yoshin-ryu Jujutsu) and named this new style of*

Karate-Do, 'Wado-Ryu' meaning: 'Japanese-way school' or also 'Peaceful-way school' since the Kanji lettering for 'Wa' can mean both.'

Ohtsuka considered the founder of Yoshin Ryu Jujutsu (Hakuda) to be the originator of his style of Karate.

Yukiyoshi Takamura, head of the Takamura Ha Shindo Yoshin Ryu Jujutsu, a branch of the ryu descended through from Shigeta Ohbata, said in *Aikido Journal* 117, Autumn 1999: *'The Wado-Ryu Jujutsu Kempo headquarters dojo still teaches Shindo Yoshin-Ryu in Tokyo. Wado-Ryu founder Hidenori Otsuka held a Menkyo Kaiden in Shindo Yoshin-Ryu. He received his license from Tatsusaburo Nakayama Sensei around 1921.*

'My grandfather knew Otsuka only slightly but thought highly of him. He was a man of exceptional reputation.

'I hope that Wado-Ryu does not lose its Jujutsu roots which makes it one of very few Karate styles to have a Bujutsu heritage.'

When he died in 1982, Ohtsuka's son Jiro took the name Hironori Ohtsuka II and succeeded him as head-master of Wado Ryu.

Shizuya Sato (1929-2011) was assistant to Ohtsuka Sensei in the 1950s. Sato also trained in Judo with Mifune and Ito, in Kendo with Nakayama and in Aikido with Kenji Tomiki. Born in 1929 in Tokyo, Japan, Sato began his lifetime study of Judo during middle school at age 12. Sato's father learnt Judo while in the Imperial Japanese Navy during World War I, and was a senior Judo instructor for the Tokyo Metropolitan Police. Sato's father's friends and Judo compatriots included many preeminent pre-WWII Kodokan instructors, including Mifune Kyuzo, Nagaoka Hidekazu, Sumiyuki Kotani, and Ito Kazuo. When Sato Sr. died in 1948, the young Sato came under the care of these senior Judoka who lent their personal guidance and lifelong support, which greatly influenced the development of Nihon Jujutsu.

Upon graduation from Meiji Gakuin University in 1948, he joined the International Section at the Kodokan. Prior to the end of WWII, in 1945, regular Kodokan training included self defence, kata, randori (sparring), taihojutsu, and, to a limited extent, weapons training such as Kenjutsu, Jojutsu, Tanbo, and Bojutsu. This multi-disciplinary approach was in keeping with Kano Jigoro's philosophy that Budo naturally evolves and grows in accordance with human experience. Postwar, a large number of non-Japanese entered the Kodokan for the first time. The majority of these young men, along with a few women, were US military personnel of the Occupation forces. Many established lifelong bonds of friendship and cooperation with Sato-Sensei and other Budo instructors, and some eventually became the pioneers responsible for introducing Japanese martial arts to the West. Significant American Budoka who began their studies at the Kodokan, and later played large roles in the ensuing development of Budo worldwide, particularly in North America, include Donn Draeger, Dan Ivan, and Walter Todd.

The core curriculum of Nihon Jujutsu incorporates the practical, decisive throwing, choking, and immobilisation methods of Judo; the entering and striking of Aikibujutsu; the restraining techniques of taihojutsu; and the taisabaki (evasive movement), open hand, and armed self-defence principles expounded by Dr.

Tomiki Kenji. When Tomiki became the Aikido director of the Kodokan's Strategic Air Command (SAC) martial arts program (1952 – 1956), Sato became the assistant Aikido instructor, and remained so for the duration of the program.

Until mid-WWII, Aikibujutsu hand-to-hand combat instruction (as directed by Ueshiba Morihei, and Tomiki Kenji, in Japan and Manchuria respectively, as well as other instructors) comprised the core of combative training for elite Imperial Japanese military personnel. During this period, the fundamental methods of Aikibutsu, Kodokan Goshin Jutsu, and Aikido were refined and compiled.

While Tomiki taught the Imperial military in Manchuria, Ueshiba Morihei directed training in Tokyo at the Toyama School (Army officer training school), the Nakano School (site of the famous Army intelligence officers' program), and at the Navy officer candidate school in Etajima.

In 1952, the US Air Force Strategic Air Command (SAC) sent two initial groups of airmen to the Kodokan to study Judo, Karatedo, Aikido, and police techniques. This program was expanded through 1956, and by its end hundreds of US Air Force martial arts instructors had trained under Sato Sensei, who instructed both Aikido (under head Aikido instructor Tomiki) and taihojutsu techniques (under taihojutsu head instructor and senior Tokyo Metropolitan Police Taihojutsu /Judo instructor Hosokawa Kusuo).

In the early 1950s, Sato Sensei began teaching Judo and self-defence at US military facilities around Tokyo.

In 1957, Sato Sensei founded the US Embassy Judo Club, where he continued to develop and refine the techniques that ultimately evolved into his Nihon Jujutsu.

Fumio Demura told me that he too studied at this site and was keen to point out that he considered Shizuya Sato was teaching Judo rather than Jujutsu. I suspect that after Jun Osano and Minoru Mochizuki, previous heads of the Nihon Jujutsu division, left Kokusai Budoin, Shizuya Sato took the job on himself. It was at this point that the Nihon Jujutsu division became essentially the practice of pre-war Judo and Tomiki Aikido.

Minoru Mochizuki was born April 7, 1907 in Shizuoka. His grandfather was the last descendant of a line of samurai and taught Kenjutsu.

Mochizuki began his martial arts training in around the 1910s. His first style was Gyokushin Ryu Jujutsu under the grandmaster Sanjuro Oshima. After this he studied many other arts, but in his advanced years, recognised as a 9th dan Nihon Jujutsu by IMAF, he tried to assemble all his knowledge into bringing back Gyokushin Ryu and wrote a manual on Nihon-den Jujutsu.

Mochizuki's first Judo teacher was Toku Sanpo. Because Toku was Okinawan and was known to perform breaking demonstrations it is not too much of a stretch to think he may have taught Mochizuki Karate as well. Although Toku was feared and revered, Kyuzo Mifune was held in even greater regard and he became Mochizuki's next teacher. The young Mochizuki even came to the attention of Judo founder Jigoro Kano, who asked Mochizuki to go and learn other arts and bring his knowledge back to the Kodokan.

Minoru Mochizuki held a 9th Dan in Nihon Jujutsu and classical scrolls in Gyokushin Ryu. [Public Domain]

Mochizuki went to study Daito Ryu Aikijujutsu under Morihei Ueshiba and stayed a student of Ueshiba all of his life. Mochizuki was awarded a mokuroku (similar to 2nd or 3rd dan) in Daito Ryu and later awarded the 10th dan Aikido by IMAF on the authority of the Ueshiba family.

Mochizuki's Karate studies are not so well documented but it has been claimed he trained with Gichin Funakoshi and may have received the grade of 5th dan. Mochizuki taught the first ever European Karateka and among the first European Aikidoka in Jean Alcheik and Claude Urvois, and later he sent Hiroo Mochizuki, Mitsuhiro Kondo (9th dan IMAF), Shoji Sugiyama and Tetsuji Murikami to teach in Europe.

Mochizuki studied at Japan's oldest extant martial arts school, the Tenshin Shoden Katori Shinto Ryu, and so impressed the headteacher that according to some sources he was offered marriage to the head-master's daughter so he could become the new Soke. Mochizuki also held the Budo grade of 8th dan in Kendo. Mochizuki studied Muso Shinden Ryu with Hakudo Nakayama (10th dan IMAF) and achieved the grade of 8th dan.

Mochizuki trained under head-master Takeji Shimazu in Shindo Muso Ryu (a school focussed around the Jo) and attained the grade of 5th dan.

Jujutsu Finds a New Home: Liverpool

While it seems that London and the South was the main martial arts scene in the UK, there was also very significant Jujutsu activity in Liverpool. We have already seen that by 1924 Harry H Hunter had a Jujutsu dojo in Liverpool.

Jack Britten, born in 1889, was a boxer in his youth in London. There are little in the way of contemporary references to Britten but an article published in the *Liverpool Echo* in 1971 reported that Britten had started Jujutsu in 1910. The story passed down is that Britten witnessed a demonstration of Jujutsu by a couple of Japanese Jujutsuka, and being rather cocky and self-assured he challenged them to a contest. It is not clear exactly who were performing the demonstration but it is known that Gunji Koizumi and Akitaro Ono were performing Jujutsu demonstrations at the 1910 Anglo-Japanese exhibition held at the White City in Shepherd's Bush, London.

The story goes that one of the Japanese gentlemen put Jack on his backside. Surprised, Jack challenged the Japanese Jujutsuka again, and was once again put on his backside. At this point Jack was offered the chance to learn Jujutsu.

Mick Walsh, a former student of Britten, told Dave Williams of the Budokan Jujitsu Club that one of Britten's instructors had committed suicide by gassing himself. This certainly suggests Koizumi may have been an instructor of Britten's.

According to another of Britten's former students, Britten had achieved 'Master' grade in Jujutsu and was teaching by 1913. There is virtually no record of Britten's training.

An article for the martial arts blog site USAdojo.com by former student Ronnie Colwell stated that Britten trained at the Anglo-Japanese School with Tani and Uyenishi. However, we know this can't be the case. Tani didn't teach at the Anglo-Japanese (more below), and by 1910 Uyenishi had long since left the UK. According to the USAdojo article by Colwell, Jack Britten fought in WWI (1914 – 1918) and was involved in hand to hand combat in the trenches, where he suffered a bayonet wound in his hand. Following the end of the war he returned to England and spent some time searching for work, until some time in 1924 he moved to Liverpool and opened the Alpha Ju Jitsu Institute.

At this point I would like to highlight a potential influence on Britten's Jujutsu. Rather than wear the more common Judo black belt, Britten wore a broad black sash and black shorts but with a white gi jacket. Tani, Uyenishi and the other Japanese practising in the UK generally wore a belt. However, the broad black sash and black shorts were also worn by Harry H Hunter, and we know that both were in Liverpool by 1924.

We know that in 1907 the Dai Nippon Butoku Kai (DNBK) had agreed to Jigoro Kano's request to changes to the uniform and had agreed to replace the sash with the belt. It is possible however that some decided to stay with the sash, or that news of the change was slow to reach some quarters. Britten wore the sash for the rest of his life. There is no further evidence to support this claim, but is it possible Britten learned some Jujutsu from Hunter? Also, does the 'Master' grade suggest Jack Britten was a member of the BJJS?

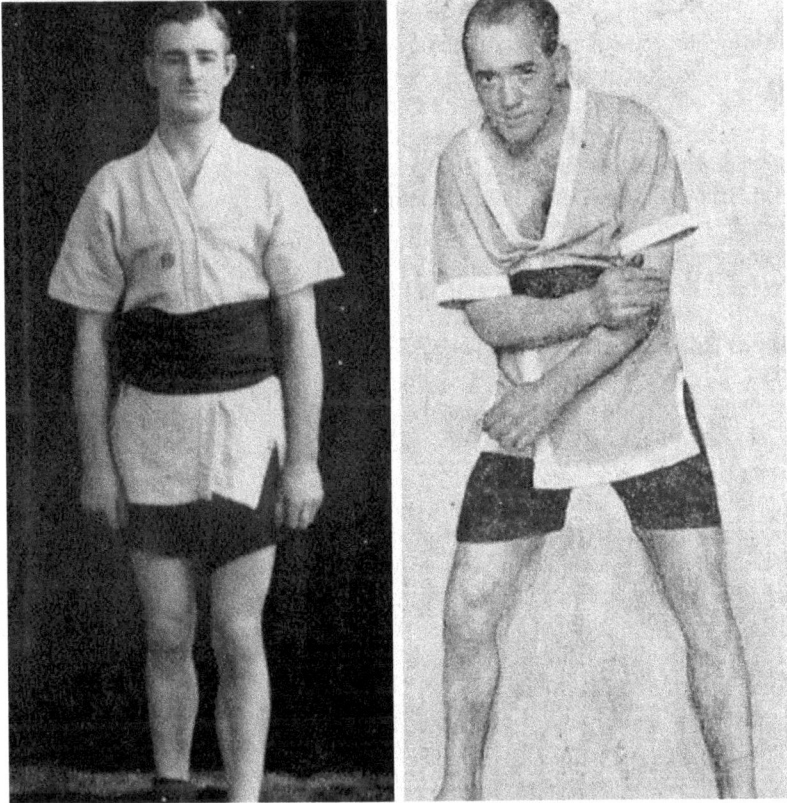

Picture of Harry Hunter (left) from Super Jujitsu (1927), and Jack Britten (right). Note the similarity of the training uniform, in particular the black sash and shorts

In the newspaper archives the first record of Jack Britten teaching Jujutsu appears to be the 16th November 1945 in the *Liverpool Echo* where he was advertising classes at 'THE JU-JITSU SCHOOL (Est. 1924)' on Smithdown Road, Liverpool. A subsequent advert in the *Liverpool Echo* on the 19th September 1950 is advertising Britten's classes at 'THE ALPHA JU-JITSU SCHOOL', still at Smithdown Road. Some time after this Britten's dojo moved to Sheil Road.

Post-war there had been a huge increase in the popularity of Judo, with large numbers of clubs developing and affiliating to the Budokwai. However, not everyone wanted to convert to Judo. Indeed, as noted in Richard Bowen's *100 Years of Judo in Great Britain, Volume 2*, at a BJA general meeting on the 1st of October 1950 apologies were noted from the Alpha Ju Jitsu Association; that is, they were invited but refused to attend. It is curious to note however that there is no direct mention of Jack Britten in either of Richard Bowen's volumes of *100 Years of Judo in Great Britain*.

There are many well-known martial artists who passed through the Alpha Ju Jitsu Institute in Liverpool. An early notable student was Francis (Frank) Beatty. Frank Beatty was born in Liverpool on the 27th of February 1924. In 1942, at age 18, Frank signed up for the war effort and served in Europe and the Far East. Within the army Frank learned some unarmed combat techniques. In 1948 Frank left the army and returned to Liverpool and at this time he became a student of Jack Britten at the Alpha. Frank would grade to 3rd dan with Jack Britten before joining the Budo of Great Britain association led by Reg Bleakman from Birmingham. In 1962 Bleakman was an area representative of the British Judo Council. Frank however remained friends with Jack Britten, and, according to former Britten student Mick Walsh, was a frequent visitor to the Alpha. Beatty also worked as a drayman (delivered barrels of beer to pubs) and was reputedly as strong as an ox. Another student of Jack Britten's was a William (Billy) Johnson, who started training with Britten in around 1966. Johnson was also a student of another Britten protégé Fred Kelly, and would subsequently become a student of Frank Beatty.

Robert Clark (see below), trained with Britten for a short period before he left and went to train with James Blundell. Eric Marshall (see below) also trained with Jack Britten for a short period. Another student of Jack's was Jimmy Pape (we will meet two men thus named, this one is 'of Chester' and the other 'Liverpool') who ultimately left the Alpha Institute and set up a Jujutsu club in Chester. It appears Jimmy and Jack Britten remained close however, as Jack would visit the Chester dojo.

An insight into Jimmy Pape's (Chester) club is provided by former student John Brunskill who recalled: *'I joined the Chester Club in 1974 and trained for 3-4 years ending up as 2nd kyu. The club located in the Oddfellows hall and was a permanent dojo with 2 good sized mats on the first floor and a further mat in the basement (scary like all good basements should be). I think the dojo was open 5 days a week, but I'm not sure. Men and women where taught separately with a slightly different syllabus. Sensei Pape was in his fifties at that time, short in height and what might be described as portly. Having said that he would lead the class in the warm up and do all the exercises out performing many of the students. To my knowledge, there was no junior class. I don't have any real memory of Jack Britten's visits; he certainly didn't go on the mat as he was blind! We were told he had an accident with bleach in a basin which he thought was water and washed his face. I guess he was in his eighties at that time. Kyu gradings where held in Chester but dan gradings where held in London. As far as I was aware there was no direct connection with Japan. The senior student at that time was Barry Williams, he was tall and a brilliant martial artist and was in his early 30s at that time. Ricky Blundell who is now the head of this group, was also training at this time but was a couple of years ahead of me, I don't think I ever trained with him as he went on different nights.'* We hear more from John Brunskill later. Another student of the Alpha was Mick Walsh, who started

70

training with Jack Britten in 1966 and became a senior instructor. Mick Walsh left the Alpha Institute in 1983 and established the Budokan Ju Jitsu club. Jimmy Davison continued to teach at the Alpha Ju Jitsu Institute after Jack Britten's death in 1978.

Another student of Jack Britten's was Ronnie Colwell. According to Ronnie Colwell (in private correspondence with myself) he started training with Jack Britten in 1953. By the mid 1960s Colwell was teaching a Jujutsu class in Southport, where he also taught what he called Kempo or Karate.

At this point it is unlikely Mr Colwell had studied actual Karate (but clearly was adept in Jujutsu) as he is not listed as a member of the British Karate Federation before 1964. Therefore it is likely his 'Karate' was actually the atemi waza of Judo/Jujutsu. What is clear however is that Colwell had firm friendships with a number of elite Karateka who respected him as a hard man and knowledgeable teacher. These include Shotokan teacher Terry O'Neill, freestyle pioneer Alfie Lewis and Goju Ryu teacher Gary Spiers. This peer group of feared and respected Karateka shows the the regard in which Colwell was held.

Since Ronnie Colwell had been teaching Karate in the early 1960s, I asked him if in his opinion he had been taught Karate by Britten. He said it didn't matter as it was all Budo and suggested he trained at around the same time as Andy Sherry (who in 1961 was a green belt under Jack Britten).

Mr Colwell's words were: "As with Andy Sherry we were Budo training. In those days we called it kenpo." Of Sherry, he added: "We both trained together with Jack. We trained together a long time."

I pressed Mr Colwell as to whether Britten had actually studied Karate (in the sense of it being Okinawan Karate or whether it was just Jujutsu strikes) and he replied: "not so sure but believe it was Okinawan. The Jujutsu taught then was what was at that time taught in Japan."

I asked Mr Colwell about the relationship between Skyner and Britten and he replied: "I came across Mr Skyner. He ran a Jujutsu club in a basement in Catharine Street, Liverpool.

"Regarding Mr Jack Britten he opened his Alpha JuJitsu Club in Smithdown Place Liverpool in 1922, later moving it to Shiel Road, Liverpool.

"Indeed they [Britten and Skyner] knew of each other but were not on [friendly] terms. Mr Skyner claimed that his Jujutsu came from Mr Kawaishi and Mr Britten being originally from London was a member of the first Ju Jitsu Society in England, being the Anglo Japanese Ju Jitsu Society under famous Japanese Instructors as Tani and Uenishi."

He added that of the Liverpool Jujutsu instructors of the 1950s, he thought Jack Britten was the best with the exception of a K Yoshida.

Colwell's son, Andrew Colwell, tells an interesting story about his father: *'My dad became friendly with a guy working as a dockhand, who was an ostracised member of the Japanese royal family - he had refused to marry someone. He was Dad's initial introduction to martial arts. He spent time with him and taught him.'*

According to Ronnie Colwell (in private correspondence with myself) this royal dockhand was a 'K Yoshida.'

Ronnie Colwell at his Southport dojo in 1962. Note, the banner on the wall in the centre says Karate. [Picture provided by Andrew Colwell]

Research reveals that there was indeed a member of the Japanese royal family who lived in Liverpool who fits this description, and so it is plausible that Colwell was friendly with him. Kanso Yoshida was a Japanese-born British seaman. He was related to Japanese Emperor Hirohito by marriage and was a resident of Liverpool from 1938. Yoshida was born in Japan, a second cousin of Princess Chichibu. He came to England in 1912, but why he left Japan is unknown. He was a ship's fireman (this means he shovelled coal into the furnace, not that he was a firefighter) by trade, and began calling himself Paddy Murphy when he realised that his Japanese name was causing him to be passed over for assignment to ships.

Yoshida served in the British merchant navy during both world wars. During WWI he was on the ship Huntstrick when it was torpedoed off Gibraltar and sank. Badly wounded in the attack, he was left with a large scar on his face. During WWII, his ship was bombed twice but he was not injured. Yoshida became a naturalised British citizen in 1940.

Of course the local newspapers and local history books of the time found it hilarious that not only was a relative of Hirohito living in Liverpool but so was a relative of Hitler! William Patrick Hitler (later changed his name to Houston for obvious reasons), son of Hitler's half-brother Alois, lived in Liverpool; therefore the headlines told of 'Paddy Yoshida and Paddy Hitler', two men related to our imperial enemies given the most comically scouse-Irish name of Paddy.

There is no evidence that Yoshida was particularly expert in any martial arts, but it gives an interesting perspective of a piece of Japanese Imperial culture that was living and breathing in Liverpool at a time when men like Ronnie Colwell (and James Blundell, see below) were working on the docks.

72

Ronnie Colwell would go on to be awarded senior grades in Karate and Jujutsu. He passed away in 2015.

Jack Britten timeline

1889: Jack Britten is born in London

1910: According to article in the *Liverpool Echo* from the 17th August 1971, Jack Britten started training in 1910. Folklore suggests it was after witnessing a demonstration of Jujutsu by two Japanese (maybe Koizumi and Ono at the Anglo-Japanese exhibition of 1910). Indirect evidence suggests Koizumi may have been an instructor of Britten.

1914 – 1918: Jack Britten fights in the trenches during WWI (story told by R Colwell).

1924: Britten moves to Liverpool to teach at the Alpha Ju-Jitsu Institute (evidence in photographs and newspaper adverts suggesting establishment in 1924) at Smithdown Road. Photographic evidence provided that suggests a potential influence from Harry Hunter, also teaching Jujutsu in Liverpool at this time.

1945 – 1950: Articles in the *Liverpool Echo* advertising the Alpha Ju-Jitsu School, still present on Smithdown Road. At some time after this the Alpha moves to Shiel Road.

1948: Upon leaving the army Frank Beatty starts learning Jujutsu from Jack Britten at the Alpha Ju-Jitsu Institute.

1951: Minutes from the BJA meeting at the Budokwai from the 1st October noting apologies from the Alpha Ju-Jitsu Association.

1950s – 1960s: Jack Britten trains notable students such as Jimmy Pape (Chester), Fred Kelly, Ronnie Colwell, Mick Walsh.

Late 1960s: Eric Marshall and Robert (Bob) Clark train at the Alpha Ju-Jitsu Institute for a brief period before moving to train with James Blundell.

Late 1960s / early 1970s: Fred Kelly starts teaching Jujutsu at the Red Triangle club in Liverpool. Jimmy Pape (Chester) establishes a club in Chester. Photographic evidence from 1974 shows Pape and Kelly wearing Juko Kai badges on their gis at the Lowlands with James Blundell.

1970s: Ronnie Colwell becomes a chief instructor at the Lowlands under James Blundell for a period, and also teaches at Skyner's Ju-Jitsu following Gerald Skyner's death (see below).

1978: Jack Britten dies aged 89.

PROF. JACK BRITTEN B.B.H.

Early portrait of Jack Britten wearing Jujutsu clothing. BBH presumably stands for 'black belt holder' [Picture provided by Dave Williams of the Budokan Ju-Jitsu Club]

THE ALPHA JU-JITSU INSTITUTE
(Established 1924)

PROF. JACK BRITTEN B.B.H.
FOUNDER & PRINCIPAL INSTRUCTOR
(BLACK BELT)

Holder of the Black Sash, (Master Grade)

Late Instructor to Members of : The London Metropolitan Police
Force, The Camberwell College of Physical Culture, Etc.

(Special Classes for Ladies)

SHEIL ROAD — LIVERPOOL 6

No connection with other clubs

A notice for the Alpha Ju-Jitsu Institute.
[Image with permission from Dave Williams of the Budokan Ju-Jitsu club]

Ronnie Colwell at his Southport dojo in 1962. Note, the banner on the
wall in the centre says Karate and Jujitsu on the right.
[Picture provided by Andrew Colwell]

Mikonosuke Kawaishi Comes To Liverpool

The Alpha Ju-Jitsu Institute was not the only Jujutsu school in Liverpool. Another was the Kawaishi Ryu run by Gerald Skyner.

Skyner claimed his Jujutsu school had been established in Liverpool in 1928 at 67 Mount Pleasant, and was originally called the Liverpool Ju Jitsu School. This would make it one of the oldest Jujutsu schools in the country.

Kawaishi in Liverpool in the 1930s

I have found press cuttings as far back as 1933 confirming Skyner's teaching in the area. Skyner's school is often associated with Mikonosuke Kawaishi (1899 – 1969). However, Kawaishi did not arrive in the UK until 1931, so if Skyner was teaching in 1928, then who taught Skyner initially?

It is possible he initially trained under Harry H Hunter? A letterhead from Skyner's dojo in 1936 recorded in Bowen's *100 Years of Judo in Great Britain, Volume 2* promotes 'expert tuition in Super Jiu Jitsu'. Could Skyner also have been a student of the 'Super Jujitsu' of Harry H Hunter?

It is possible; Hunter left the UK for Canada in 1929, coinciding with Skyner starting to teach Jujutsu in Liverpool in 1928.

Mikonosuke Kawaishi studied Judo under Isogai Hajime, and also studied Aikijujutsu under Yoshida Kotaro while training at the Dai Nippon Butoku Kai's Butokuden. Kawaishi also studied Judo in Kyoto with Master Tomio Kurihara (the 11th man to be awarded 10th dan by the Kodokan).

Yoshida Kotaro (1883-1966) is a fascinating character. Not only was he a master of Daito Ryu Aikijujutsu, he was also the inheritor of his own family style of Aikijujutsu Yanagi Ryu, a member of the notorious Black Dragon Society, and the man who introduced the founder of Aikido, Morihei Ueshiba, to his teacher Sokaku Takeda.

Kawaishi left Japan for the USA in the 1920s. In 1927 Kawaishi established the New York Judo Club. Before that he had been a professional wrestler in San Diego from 1926-1927. Kawaishi had initially arrived in Seattle on May 17, 1926, on the merchant vessel Paris Maru, which had sailed out of Kobe with just two passengers aboard. Kawaishi listed his occupation as student. His fellow passenger was Shigeru Yoshitaro, who was also 26 years old.

Incidentally, if one should ever visit South Africa then it is possible to visit the Paris Maru; it ran aground there in 1934 and is now a tourist attraction.

Kawaishi arrived in the UK in 1931 and turned up at the Budokwai looking for work. Gunji Koizumi offered him work as an instructor and there are records noted by Bowen in *100 Years of Judo in Great Britain, Volume 2* showing that in 1932 the Budokwai had sent Kawaishi to Preston to assess three members of the Lancashire Constabulary.

At this time Kawaishi was 33 years old and a 4th dan. Kawaishi also became the instructor of the Budokwai affiliated Oxford University Judo Club. Bowen also records the universal dislike of Kawaishi at the Budokwai. He was known to gamble and borrow excessively and was thought to be fairly unpleasant, although a competent Judoka.

In 1932 2nd dan Charles Cawkell left the Budokwai to establish the Anglo-Japanese Judo Club at 7a Strathmore Gardens, Notting Hill Gate, London, with the help of Kawaishi. Subsequently Kawaishi left the Budokwai for the Anglo-Japanese taking the Oxford club with him, much to the displeasure of the Budokwai. The Anglo-Japanese Club was incorporated as a company and Kawaishi now supplemented his instructor's income as a professional wrestler using the stage name 'Matsuda' and would wrestle around the country, including at the Liverpool Stadium. At this time the Anglo-Japanese Club now started to rival the Budowkai as the UK's premier Judo organisation.

It is also at this time we begin to see an association between Skyner and Kawaishi. In the *Liverpool Echo* of July 22nd 1932 Skyner has an advert offering ladies Jujutsu and Judo lessons *'as taught in the Japanese Club, London, and by my past tutor, the champion of London'*. We can infer that the Japanese Club is the Anglo-Japanese, as the *Liverpool Echo*, 11th September 1934, posted an advert for 'SKYNER'S JU-JITSU SCHOOL' listing Matsuda (Kawaishi) as the principal instructor. Who the *'champion of London'* was remains a mystery, but may also have been Matsuda (Kawaishi), or possibly Jack Robinson (see below).

Kawaishi would not last long at the Ango-Japanese Club. In 1935 Kawaishi was charged and fined for assaulting a young woman called Bonita Phillips in London. This may have hastened Kawaishi's exit and he moved to Paris where he would become recognised for the development of Judo in France.

In life Kawaishi achieved the rank of 7th dan, but was awarded the rank of 10th dan posthumously by the French Judo Federation. Kawaishi would later publish several books including *My Method of Self-Defence* (1957) which gives insights into his method of Jujutsu.

It seems that Kawaishi's exit ended Skyner's relationship with the Anglo-Japanese Judo Club. A letterhead from Skyner's dojo in 1936 recorded in Bowen's *100 Years of Judo in Great Britain, Volume 2* shows that Skyner's 'LIVERPOOL JIU-JITSU AND JUDO ACADEMY' was now affiliated to the 'International and South African Jiu Jitsu Society'. The South African Jiu Jitsu Society was run by Jack Robinson.

Skyner in action.

Judo historian Tony Underwood was able to provide some more information about Jack Robinson. Robinson started to learn Judo in 1910 from his father, who had a contest with Yukio Tani in Newcastle on Tyne in 1904. Robinson claimed to have beaten both Yukio Tani and Matsutaru Otani in 1923.

He may also have been a Cumberland and Westmorland wrestling champion. In 1931 Robinson left the UK for South Africa and founded his South African Jiu Jitsu Association in 1936. A picture of Robinson with his club from this time shows him styled as Prof J S Robinson S.B.D., S.M.F., L.T.D., (Judo Shinah (presumably a misspelling of Shihan), Jiu-Jitsu Champion Great Britain, South Africa and Europe). Robinson claimed the Jujitsu Championship of the World by beating Leopold McLaglen (mentioned above). Robinson also claimed the Lightweight Championship of the British Empire, a title he lost to Billy Riley, the catch wrestler from Wigan who would establish the famous Snake Pit gym.

A dan grade certificate (for the Degree of Supreme Principal Master) from Robinson in 1936 also makes interesting reading with exam marks for 'Theory of Balance' and 'Anatomy' recorded. Jack Robinson's sons were also esteemed martial artists (Robinson had eight children, five sons). Joe Robinson was a well known Judoka and in 1955 even fought Kenshiro Abbe (see below). Tony Underwood recalled that Jack Robinson challenged the Budokwai to choose ten of their best fighters and his sons would take a line up of them. However the challenge was refused as the Robinsons were claimed to be professionals and the BJA banned professional Judoka. Robinson died in 1974, as a 10th dan. Jack Robinson produced at least one book, *Karate, Judo, Self Defence*, in South Africa, where it stated he was a 10th dan and 'Unbeaten Judo Champion of the World.'

Top Row : J. G. MENINGSOHN, B.S., Hon. Instructor.   H. JUNIPER, B.S., Donated Junior Champion, 1936.

Second Top Row: G. J. STEPHENS, A. J. A. SMITH, V.A.   C. GORDON, V.A.,   J. GORDON, V.A.,   P. SCHULZA, V.A.,   J. BURLEIGH, V.A.

Third Top Row: K. BASLIAR, B.S.,   J. BRETURNHOUT, B.S.,   J.L. SOUTTER, B.S.,   A. v. saw JUL, B.S., Gen. Instructor.   G. WAUGH, B.S., E. OLIVACK, B.S.
V. LLOYE, B.S., Hon. Instructor.

Front Row: G. SHARPSON, U.S., Gen. Instructor,   STELLA WAREIE, B.C.D., Instructress,   A. P. POURER, Hon. Instructor, Donated Champion, 1936.   S. DUCLEY, D.S., Hon. Instructor.
P.A.N. A.J.L.C. Ichampion, 1936.   E. W. H. WEEKOM, D.B. Chairman, S.A.   A. MASS, V.P., Physical Director,   F. BRADFORD, Hon. Instructor, Hon. Sec.

Bottom Row, Seated : JOHN ROBINSON, V.A.,

JOE ROBINSON, V.A.

INTERNATIONAL
JIU-JITSU SOCIETY
AND E.J.-J.A. - S.A.J.-J.S.

HEADQUARTERS
LONDON - TOKIO - BERLIN - KIOTO
OFFICIAL HEADQUARTERS: DOSHISHA COLLEGE, JAPAN.

Certificate of Degree.

Diplomas Yellow - Blue - Brown - Black Belt.

Degree Supreme Principle Master.

Theory of Balance 93 Points V.S.

Anatomy 50 Points N.T.K.

Points General 92 Points.   *Remarks* C. R. T.

Name A.A. VAN ZYL.

Address 251a, BERTHA STREET, KENILWORTH.

DATE 1/6/36.   PLACE Johannesburg, S.A.

EXAMINER *H.L. Robinson* S.B.D.
PROFESSOR OF JIUDO.

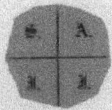

We don't know how long Skyner's association with Robinson lasted. Any association with the Ango-Japanese Judo Club ended during WWII, as on the 23rd of October 1942, most likely because of a lack of membership due to the war, the Anglo-Japanese Judo Club ceased operating as a company.

Skyner, along with his five brothers, served in WWII in the RAF, where Skyner became a military instructor, also teaching the police. Karateka and author Dennis Martin said of Skyner: *'Gerry Skyner ran a respected, hard training school in Catharine Street. I heard that Skyner was recruited to teach hand-to-hand during WWII, and only lasted one session, because, while demonstrating a counter, he smashed his "assailant" to a pulp with a steel helmet.'*

Skyner moved the club to 5 Catharine Street (perhaps after WWII) in Liverpool 8 (not to be confused with nearby Catherine Street) and it was referred to as 'Skyner's Ju Jitsu'. A Bill Woods (not the notable Judoka who trained under Abbe) wrote on a Liverpool nostalgia forum that in 1957 he was a member of Professor Gerry Skyner's BJA Judo Team, suggesting the possibility that by the 1950s or 60s Skyner's was a registered member of the British Judo Association. Senior students of Skyner's included Ray Dakin, Bill Nelson, Jack Cunningham, Bernie Gavan, Ray Davies, Ronnie Davies, Andy Howarth, and Ronnie Wright.

Bill Nelson's Navy leave pass. He was a senior student in both Gerry Skyner's Kawaishi Ryu and Gunji Koizumi's Arnot Street Judo club.

One of the earliest black belts at Skyner's in the 1940s was Bill Nelson (who was actually my great uncle). Nelson began learning hand to hand combat and boxing as a child in the 1920s-30s under his father (WWI soldier WH Nelson) and grandfather (Swedish Royal Navy sailor A Nilsson). Then, after serving in the Merchant Navy in WWII, Nelson joined Skyner's Jujutsu club. In the 1950s Nelson joined Bob Hamilton's Arnot Street Jujutsu School, which became the northern base of the British Judo Association with Gunji Koizumi himself conducting the gradings there in the 1950s.

Former Skyner student Ronnie Wright was quoted by the *Liverpool Echo* in December 2003 as saying: *'A man stopped Skyner outside the club one night and asked how long it would take him to get a black belt. Skyner told him: "Half an hour! Catch the bus at the stop over the road and go to Jack Sharps (sports shop) - they sell them there". Basically he was telling him he might never get one - there is no quick or easy way.'* Skyner did not use the terminology of kyu and dan grades. Once asked what dan grade he held, he grumpily replied: *'Every bloody dan.'*

Skyner's dojo on Catharine Street, Liverpool

Towards the end of his life Skyner would spend the day in the pub and would challenge anyone to a fight, offering them £100 if they could beat him – he never lost.

Former five time world Karate champion Alfie Lewis started his martial arts journey at Skyner's and told me about the dojo on Catharine Street: *'There was a pub on the corner called the Blackburne Arms that Mr Skyner used to drink at during class.'* Gerald Skyner died in late 1971 and his loyal students continued running the club. They hosted many visiting masters including Malaysian Budokan Karate master Chew Choo Soot and at one stage Ronnie Colwell was an instructor when the club became known as Hana Ku Ryu.

MIKIMINOSOKI KAWAISHI
CHAMPION OF JAPAN
(Matsuda of Stadium Repute)
Ex Instructor to Oxford U...

A Skyner's flier calling Kawaishi 'Matsuda of [Liverpool] stadium repute' and ex instructor to Oxford university. Note both Kawaishi and Skyner wore a conventional Judo gi and belt as opposed to the sash and shorts of Jack Britten

Skyner/Kawaishi timeline

1904/1908: Gerald Skyner is born to Mr and Mrs W Skyner. His siblings are William, Albert, Leslie, Cecil and Fred.

1928: Traditional date for founding of Skyner's 'Liverpool Ju Jitsu School'. He is in his early 20s.

1931: Kawaishi arrives at the Budokwai and becomes an instructor, also teaching at the Oxford University Judo Club.

1932: Skyner writes to the *Liverpool Echo*, where he is described as an instructor. He refers to the Japanese Club London and his 'tutor the champion of London.'

1932/1933: Kawaishi helps establish the Anglo-Japanese Judo Club in London where he becomes an instructor and leaves the Budokwai. Kawaishi also starts to wrestle for money.

1933: Skyner featured in *Liverpool Echo* (May) demonstrating the 'fascinating art of Ju-Jitsu.'

This card from Annelд's comedian explains itself.

JU-JITSU AT PICTON

The Liverpool Ju-Jitsu Club, under the direction of Professor Gerald M Skyner, hold a tournament at the Picton Hall, William Brown-street, to-night, at 7.45. The programme includes ju-jitsu contests, demonstrations of self-defence for women and men, and several humorous items; while concert artistes will also contribute. Councillor F. W Tucker, J.P., will preside.

Classified advert for Skyner

1933: The *Nottingham Evening Post* describes Kawaishi (Matsuda) as a wrestler: *'The leading supporting item, also one of ten 5-min rounds, introduces another newcomer in Matsuda, a Japanese master of the Judo style wrestling, which he liberally exploits. He opposes the popular Golden Hawk.'*

1933: *Nottingham Evening Post* describes Kawaishi (Matsuda) as: *'young Japanese Ju Jitsu expert.'* It says: *'The Japanese, who claims to have engaged in a thousand contests without defeat, has an extraordinary style. He wrestled in bare feet and used them...'*

1933: 7th December in the *Liverpool Echo* Kawaishi (Matsuda) described as *'one of the great personalities in the game'* and says he is *'a favourite with the local fans.'*

1934: *Liverpool Echo*, 11th September 1934, posted an advert for 'SKYNER'S JU-JITSU SCHOOL' listing Matsuda (Kawaishi) as the principal instructor.

1934: Kawaishi (Matsuda) wrestles in Liverpool Stadium against Jack Wentworth.

Skyner teaching the military knife defences

1934: In the *Portsmouth Evening News* on the 15th February Kawaishi (Matsuda) referred to as *'the world's greatest Ju Jitsu professor from Oxford'* when he wrestles in Portsmouth against the famous Jack Pye.

1934: In the *Press and Journal* from the 27th January Kawaishi (Matsuda) wrestles Pye in Scotland where it is reported: *'Japanese wrestler, Matsuda, the jujitsu champion of his country, who wrestled in bare feet against Jack Pye, of Doncaster, whom he beat two falls to one. The Japanese was much too clever for Pye, and the fearsome yells emitted by Matsuda every time that he threw.'*

1935: In the *Liverpool Echo* on the 22nd August Kawaishi (Matsuda) wrestles in Bristol against Clem Hosier. Matsuda headlines wrestling bills and he is described as having *'a big reputation in Liverpool.'*

1935: Skyner's demo featured in the *Liverpool Echo* (July) described as *'Ju Jitsu wrestling'* and his adverts in the *Nottingham Evening Post* describe him as *'Professor Skyner' 'England's leading expert'* and cite his teacher as *'Matsuda champion of Japan.'*

1935: Kawaishi described in the *Liverpool Echo* as: *'Matsuda the clever little Japanese wrestler.'* He wrestles at Liverpool stadium against Gary Currie, Dave Ormiston, King Kong Curtis, Cony Baer and Jack Adam. The paper says he uses *'skill over strength.'*

Skyner in action, pictures courtesy of Andy Howarth Sensei

1935: Kawaishi (Matsuda) defeated Catch Wrestling and Wigan Snakepit head Billy Riley at the Liverpool Stadium. The *Liverpool Echo* reported: *'The main bout in the free style wrestling programme at the Stadium, last night, saw Matsuda the Japanese champion, defeat Billy Riley (Wigan), the former Empire middleweight champion, by two falls to one, after an exciting bout.'*

1935: Kawaishi is charged and fined for assaulting Bonnita Phillips in London. Kawaishi leaves the Anglo-Japanese Judo Club, and the UK, moving to Paris, France.

1935: Skyner and a host of famous sportsmen featured on the BBC's *In Town To-night* programme.

1936: Reported in the *Liverpool Echo* on the 25th November, Skyner holds a Jujutsu competition at Picton Hall, William Brown Street, Liverpool.

1936: Letterhead showing Skyner's 'LIVERPOOL JIU JITSU AND JUDO ACADEMY' is now affiliated to Jack Robinson's International and South African Jiu Jitsu Society.

The six Skyner brothers when they joined military at the start of World War II.

1939-1940: Skyner advertises his *'world renowned'* system in the *Liverpool Echo* saying it *'floors bullies and ruffians like ninepins.'*

1941: Skyner and his five brothers are featured in the *Liverpool Echo* as they all serve in the war. Gerald, 37 (therefore born in around 1904) is in the RAF and described as a Ju Jitsu expert.

1943: Skyner advertises Jujutsu classes in the *Liverpool Echo* while on leave.

1944: Skyner advertises his reopened school in the *Liverpool Echo*. Bill Nelson begins training with Skyner, now at his dojo at 54 Catharine Street (the dojo would later move to 5 Catharine Street).

1945: Skyner described in the *Liverpool Echo* as an ex RAF and police instructor and in the *Lancashire Evening Post* (teaching in Preston) as a British Champion.

1947: Reported in the *Liverpool Echo* on the 6th September, Skyner does a playful demo match with his young daughter. The dojo is referred to as Skyner College.

1950: Skyner is referred to as Northern Counties Champion and gives a demo in Gloucester reported on by the *Tewkesbury Register*. He is assisted by the Alma Judo Club.

1951: The Tewkesbury paper states: *'The ju-jitsu display was given by members of the Worcester Judo School (Professor Gerald M. Skyner, the principal, who is also principal of the Liverpool School of Ju-jitsu. Instructor to the R.A.F. Police and Blackbelt.'* In another demonstration he is assisted by a Corporal Powell.

1954: Skyner's student Bill Nelson joins Bob Hamilton's Arnot Street School.

1966: A female student of Skyner's (his most senior *'girl pupil'*) is featured in the *Liverpool Echo*. The club is described as established for 33 years (therefore starting in 1932 or 1933).

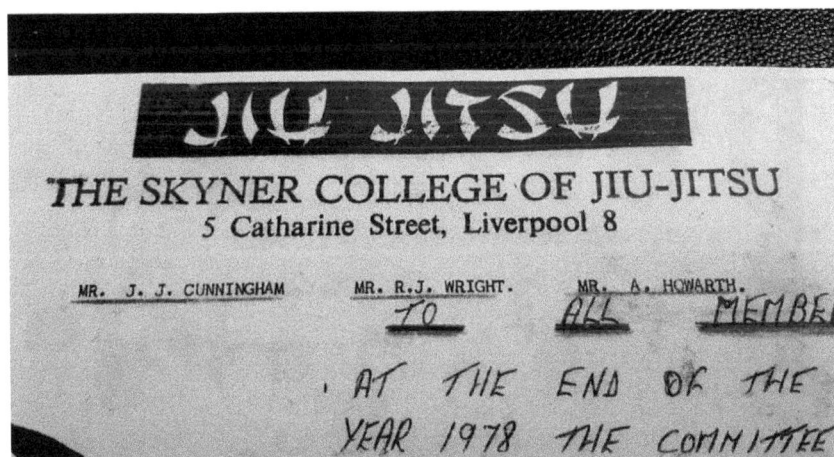

JIU JITSU

THE SKYNER COLLEGE OF JIU-JITSU
5 Catharine Street, Liverpool 8

MR. J. J. CUNNINGHAM   MR. R.J. WRIGHT.   MR. A. HOWARTH.
            TO   ALL   MEMBE[

. AT THE END OF THE
YEAR 1978 THE COMMITTEE

1971: Skyner dies, according to his obituary, aged 63 (therefore born in 1908, contrary to previously suggested year of birth as 1904). His club is later taken over by students such as Gerry Malcomson, Ronnie Davis, Ray Davis, Jack Cunningham, Ronnie Wright and Andy Howarth.

1979: Malaysian Budokan master Chew Choo Soot teaches at Skyner's.

Gunji Koizumi returned to Liverpool in the late 1940s (having previously taught at the ill-fated Kara Ashikaga in 1906 as discussed earlier), where Arnot Street School's Judo club became affiliated to the British Judo Association (BJA). BJA fliers collected by Richard Bowen, and now stored at the University of Bath, list the instructor as Jack Keersley 1st dan, with a Miss Edwards as the President. The programme for the annual Arnot Street grading of 1952/1953 lists Koizumi 7th dan as the grading examiner, Kearsley as chief instructor, and instructors T Crossley and R Hamilton.

In the previous year's programme, Kearsley was listed with Crossley and S Moran. In that year R Hamilton was listed as a 3rd kyu and in the programme performed *'a demonstration of balance and body movement known as Tsukuri.'* In 1953/1954 Kearsley, Crossley and Hamilton are listed with a J Isaacson. Robert Hamilton took over the running of the Arnot Street Judo Institute in around 1954 and Bill Nelson, previously a black belt under Gerry Skyner, joined the club.

Robert Hamilton's son of the same name told me that he believed his father took over the club in 1954: *'It might have been 1954 as I was about six then and remember helping my dad clean it up ready for the mats. My dad had a few clubs, one in Bootle, Warbreck Moor, Jacobs Factory and Arnot Street. My dad also trained at the Red Triangle Karate club with some notable champions.'*

Robert Hamilton, back row centre pictured circa 1955 in one of his Liverpool Judo clubs [Picture courtesy of Mr Hamilton's son]

MAY . 54

J U D O

Judo is a unique form of combative art; its practice provides all we consider best in sport, the promotion of mental & physical development, gratification of the competitive instinct, and the stimulation of the spirit of fair play. However the most important part of Judo is that one attains skill, one acquires physically and mentally balanced poise, self-reliance, and calm alertness.

o o o o o

NUMBERS OF BELTS.

6th KYU	White Belt.	1st Dan.	Forms of locks & holds.
5th KYU	Yellow "	2nd Dan.	Forms counter throws.
4th KYU	Orange "	3rd Dan.	Forms gentleness.
3rd KYU	Green "	4th Dan.	Forms spiritual & mental balance.
2nd KYU	Blue "	5th Dan.	Forms unity of the duality.
1st KYU	Brown "	6th Dan.	Forms the Mastership.
		7th Dan.	
		o o o o o	

JUDO CLASSES:

LADIES:	Wednesday	7-30 - 9-30 p.m.
GENTLEMEN	Monday,	" " "
	Tuesday,	" " "
	Thursday,	" " "
	Friday.	" " "

PARTICULARS NOW AVAILABLE FROM MR. CROSSLEY.

LIVERPOOL EDUCATION COMMITTEE.

ARNOT STREET EVENING INSTITUTE.

J U D O   C L U B

(Affiliated to the "Budokwai", London)
also
(Member of British Judo Association)

P R O G R A M M E

for

5th ANNUAL GRADING 1953/4.

on

Saturday, May 8th at 2-30 p.m.

in

Arnot Street School Gymnasium.

Chief Instructor:-	Mr. J. Yearsley.
Instructors:-	W. T. Crossley, S. Hamilton. J. Tennyson.
Grading Examiner:-	Mr. G. Koizumi. (7th DAN)
Dojo Stewards:-	Mrs. J. Inmanson and Messrs. K. Spofforth, E. Morley, W. Roberts.

May 1954 programme from Arnot Street listing Gunji Koizumi (7th Dan) as grading examiner and Bob Hamilton as an instructor. Leaflet courtesy of the Bowen Collection at the University of Bath

Bill Nelson's book collection may be telling as to what Jujutsu and Judo students in Liverpool circa 1944-1954 were reading. The books, passed to his great nephew, were the H Irving Hancock books *The Complete Kano Jiu Jitsu* (1905) and *Jiu Jitsu Combat Tricks* (1904). Nelson also kept a cutting from 1954 which talked about a Budokwai demo by Koizumi.

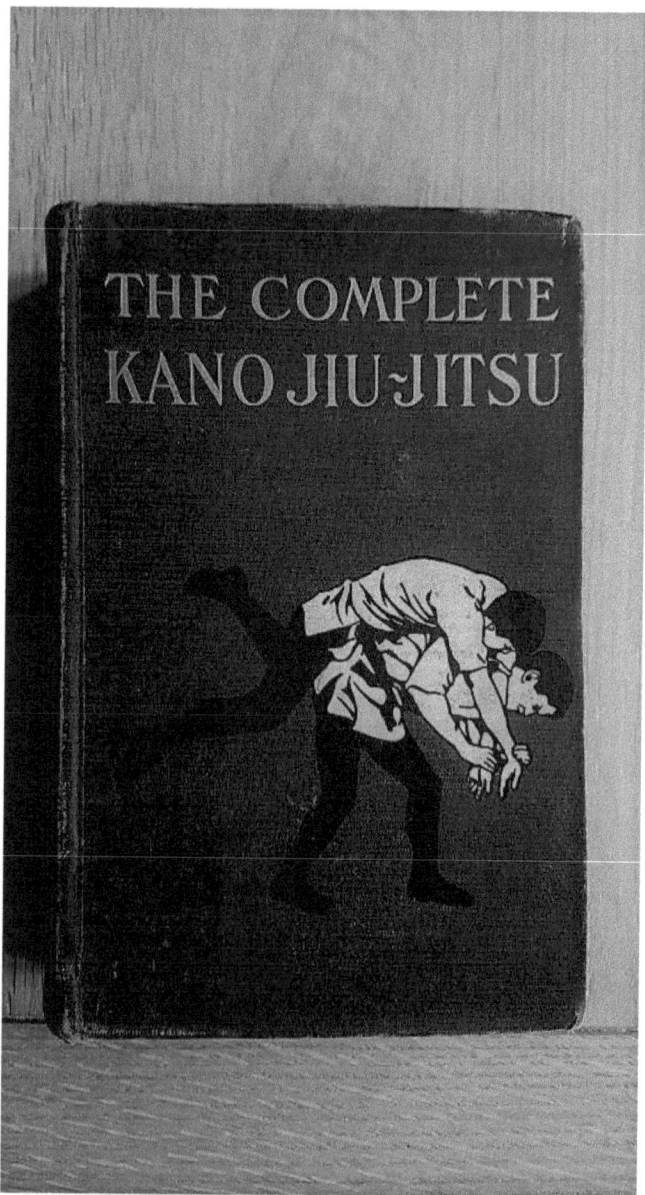

Chew Choo Soot (pictured teaching at Phil Handyside's Preston Dojo) taught at Skyner's [Picture courtesy of Phil Handyside]

Chew Choo Soot came to Britain in 1978. He stayed in Liverpool and taught at Skyner's Jujutsu, and, with the help of Preston Shotokan Karateka Phil Handyside, organised the first Karate Budokan International (KBI) World Championships. Alfie Lewis, mentioned above, competed at the event. Handyside, who began his training with Jujutsu in 1963 under Richard Butterworth, had got his 1st dan black belt in Shotokan Karate in 1977 under Hirokazu Kanazawa, and following this took his 2nd dan in Budokan under Chew Choo Soot. KBI's UK presidency was assumed by Mike Newton (with Handyside as vice president). Newton was a student of Trevor Jones, who was in turn a student of Vernon Bell (see below). In around 2003, Newton, who already held 7th dan in Budokan Karate under Chew, was awarded 7th dan in Yoseikan Karate, Jujutsu and Kobudo by Bell. It is also worth noting that former Alpha Institute senior Mick Walsh, after the death of Jack Britten associated with Chew Choo Soot, joined the KBI and called his club the Budokan Ju Jitsu Club.

What was to become a Liverpool based Jujutsu school of great importance in the UK was established by James Blundell.

James Blundell's BJJA

James Blundell at the Lowlands
[Picture with permission from Wayne Blundell]

On Wednesday, 21st December 1921, James Joseph Blundell was born. From a young age James was determined to go to sea and (age 14) lied about his age to join the merchant navy. In the years before WWII James travelled the world with the merchant navy and made many visits to the far east. When his ship was in dock James would spend his spare time investigating local areas and their martial arts systems, which fascinated him. This was not merely a passing interest, it was a passion, and James recorded every technique he learnt. Some literature suggests that in Singapore while on shore leave James learnt martial arts from a Chinese gentleman called Master Kim. Cataloguing his experiences in this way was to become instrumental in the development of Jujutsu later in his life. James was not particular about specific martial arts, or their origin, and he learned and recorded techniques from Japanese and Chinese styles.

At the outbreak of WWII Britain's merchant navy was the biggest in the world, and was tasked with transporting goods or soldiers - it was critical for the war effort. Such was its importance the German Navy made it a target, and even with Royal Navy protection the merchant navy suffered high losses. James did not escape. During WWII James was torpedoed twice, firstly by a German U-Boat, in the North Atlantic, and the second time by a Japanese submarine. After the second attack he was adrift on a lifeboat with fifteen other men for ten days. Of the fifteen James was one of only two survivors. During WWII James Blundell may also have learned combatives developed by Fairbairn.

Following the war James found employment with the Mersey Docks and Harbour Company on a salvage vessel. Now, with the horror of war behind him, James could resume his passion for martial arts. In 1952 James Blundell became a trustee of a mansion at 13 Haymans Green, West Derby Village, in Liverpool, called the Lowlands. James used the basement of the Lowlands to start teaching Jujutsu, firstly to the upper echelons of Liverpool society, and subsequently to everyone who wanted to learn. In 1956 James had the foresight to establish the British Ju Jitsu Association (BJJA). He formed the BJJA to embrace the different Jujutsu schools and styles of the era and to promote Jujutsu. David Brough told me that James's son Kenny Blundell had mentioned in conversation that fellow Liverpool Jujutsuka Jack Britten and Gerald Skyner were invited to join but declined, happy to follow their respective paths. Interestingly, during this period part of the basement was also used as a nightclub, called the Pillar club, which was apparently even frequented by the Beatles before their stardom. Following the closure of the Pillar club James Blundell converted the whole of the basement of the Lowlands into his dojo.

James Blundell had also studied Jujutsu in Liverpool with William Green, who was a student of Harry H Hunter mentioned above (this may have been Benjamin Green, who appeared in Hunter's book *Super Jujitsu*). However, James didn't really consider that he ever had one main instructor, but that he had many, and he assimilated techniques from all of them. Another influence on James Blundell's Jujutsu was Uyenishi's *The Text Book of Ju-Jutsu as Practised in Japan*. Robert Ashworth (see below), who was a student of James Blundell, told David Brough who told me that James Blundell worked from the book of Uyenishi to organise his syllabus. This is an important insight as it sheds light on the origin of some of the BJJA syllabus.

The terminology used in Uyenishi's *Text book of Ju Jutsu* bears a striking similarity to the terminology used in British Jujutsu. For example, while stomach throw, scissors, and shoulder throw are used, the term 'hock' is also introduced. The image below is from Uyenishi's book (1905) and shows Uyenishi demonstrating what he describes as a 'Cross hook' or a 'Hock hook'. It seems reasonable to suggest that this specific terminology was further simplified to what is known today in British Jujutsu as a 'Cross hock'.

95

Uyenishi performing a cross hock from 'The Text Book of Ju Jutsu as Practised in Japan' (1905, public domain). The term 'hock' is fairly unique to British Jujutsu.

Further insight into the Jujutsu taught by Uyenishi can be found in the books of his students, such as his senior student William Garrud. As mentioned above Garrud authored *The Complete Jujitsuan* (1914). In *The Complete Jujitsuan* Garrud sets out Jujutsu counters and techniques in response to a number of different attack scenarios. These different scenarios and defences were instantly recognisable to BJJA(GB) historian David Brough, who holds a 3rd dan in a derivative of Blundell's syllabus (see below).

As mentioned above, James Blundell had also (according to James Shortt) been a student of Green, who had been a student of Harry H Hunter, author of *Super Jujitsu* (1927). Thus might we also expect to see an influence of Super Jujitsu within the Blundell syllabus? Indeed, BJJA(GB) historian David Brough thinks this is the case.

The Lowlands, an important home of British Jujutsu.
[Picture taken by David Brough]

As stated above, in the early 1930s there was an association between Gerald Skyner and Mikonosuke Kawaishi. David Brough also thinks that applications presented in Kawaishi's *My Method of Self-Defence* (1957) also form part of the core British Jujutsu syllabus. Thus we can infer that Kawaishi and his work was also influential. In conversations with many British Jujutsuka in the preparation of this book it has been suggested that the commonly applied defences to punches are an influence of Karate.

It is my opinion however that this is not the case. What we see in the works of Garrud and Hunter are chapters dedicated to the use of Jujutsu against boxing. That is, Jujutsu defences against punches. This is an important adaption of the Jujutsu taught by Uyenishi to a British fighting style, and indeed was even present in the early 1900 articles written by Barton-Wright. This marks a departure of British Jujutsu from Judo of the time, in that throws were now

97

executed from punches as opposed to the more common grip. It also leads to the development of British Jujutsu into a more counter-attacking style of martial art.

Thus in the development of his syllabus James Blundell preserved the legacy of Uyenishi, his students, and the BJJS, which would now live on through Blundell's BJJA. James organised the techniques into a layered syllabus from white to black belt, organised in levels of increasing difficulty.

While this seems obvious today, at the time this structure in British Jujutsu had been lacking. Eric Marshall, who started learning Jujutsu in 1965 with Gerald Skyner student Bert Roberts at a club in Stanley House, Upper Parliament Street, Liverpool, and who had also trained at the dojo[s] of Britten and Skyner before going to James Blundell's, recalled that at the time black belts were achieved after a period of dedicated training and demonstrating, rather than having any structure.

The original BJJA badge still hanging on the wall of the Lowlands dojo.
[Picture provided by Wayne Blundell]

James Blundell's older brother, Bernie Blundell, was also a Jujutsu instructor (and later a 6th dan with the BJJA). Bernie Blundell opened a Jujutsu club in Kirkby in around 1959 at Southdene Community Centre. Other brother John Blundell may have also taught there.

David Keegan, my father, trained at the Kirby dojo when it opened, and recalls the formal opening was conducted by future Prime Minister Harold Wilson!

David, who joined the club with his twin brother Paul, said: *'I was born in 1950 and took up my first martial art aged 9 or 10 so it was about 1959-1960. We lived in Kirkby near Liverpool and we were in the Scouts at the time but we had to walk one and a half miles to get to class. Then we had the opportunity to take up Jujutsu which was only a quarter of a mile away and only cost six pence. The instructor was Sensei Blundell, the brother of Liverpool Jujutsu pioneer Jim Blundell. He was the real deal, he was no wimp. He stood there in his gi and blackbelt and had a great charismatic personality. He showed every technique by example, sometimes with the assistance of older students. There was a lot of running and circuit training to begin with and then breakfalls, both sides then back – a great deal of breakfalls. We had no mats and just had to take our shoes off. Then we progressed to running rolls, then the shoulder throws and hip throws. We'd learn a throw then do the counter.'*

In circa 1959 martial arts in Liverpool were not commonplace, with David Keegan stating: *'The only martial arts were Jujutsu at our club then St Chads had Judo and there was a few old fashioned boxing clubs. John Conteh (future British boxing champion) was in my class at school and he trained with Kirkby ABA. There was never anything on telly about martial arts back then, just boxing and wrestling and we'd go to Liverpool Stadium on a Friday night and watch wrestling – which were more like real fights than today – with the likes of Jack Pye and Billy Two Rivers. Even the American boxers used to train at Liverpool Stadium when they were over here and we could go and see them train.'*

After studying Jujutsu and Tibetan meditation, David Keegan trained with members of the Red Triangle Karate Club. My father first introduced me to Karate and Jujutsu and later pursued Chinese martial arts. His studies came full circle when he trained in Muso Jikiden Eishin Ryu with teachers including Allan Tattersall who had also begun his training with the Blundells.

James Blundell's style, and reputation as a teacher, grew, and people would travel from far and wide to learn his Jujutsu. Robert (Bob) Clark joined the Lowlands in the 1960s after a period at Jack Britten's dojo. A grading book issued in 1967 shows that James Blundell was the Chairman, G. A. Mason was the Vice-chairman, G. Griffiths was the Honorary Secretary, and B. Blundell was the Treasurer. Also listed are members of the Committee: John Blundell, W. Maguire, and R. Colwell.

A newspaper article dated July 24th 1969 about the Lowlands lists James Blundell as 6th dan and Alan Mason as 2nd dan with Bob Clark highlighted as a brown belt. Bob Clark would rise quickly to apparently become James Blundell's senior student.

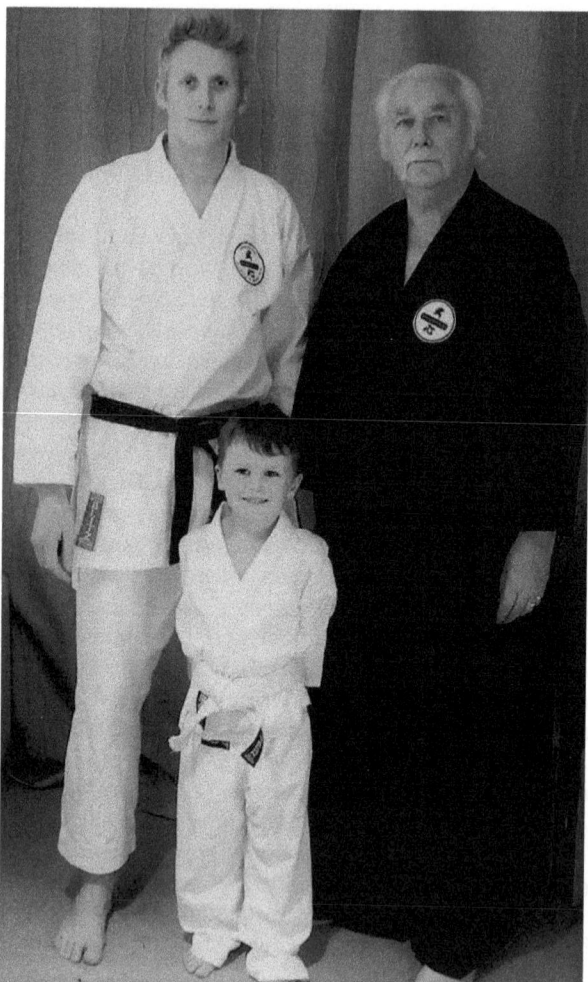

David Keegan who first studied Jujutsu in around 1959 under the Blundells. With son Simon Keegan (the author) and grandson Edward Keegan.

In 1970 James affiliated his BJJA to the American based Jujutsuka Rodney Sacharnoski and his Juko Kai organisation (Ju Jitsu Black Belt Federation of America – JJBBFA) which formed the first incarnation of the World Ju Jitsu Federation. Sacharnoski's WJJF was formed in 1970 by Sacharnoski, Albert Church, and H. Olsen. At this time Blundell's style adopted the name Juko Ryu and members of the BJJA wore the Juko Kai badge on their gi (training uniform). A BJJA grading book from 1975 shows that at this time Sacharnoski was 'Soke' of the World Ju Jitsu Federation incorporating the BJJA, of which James Blundell was Chairman and a 7th dan. The International and North of England Secretary was W. B. Fenner, 3rd dan. Sacharnoski's Juko Kai organisation would subsequently award James Blundell a 'Sokeship' and the title of Soke in 1978 for the development of his style.

A BJJA letterhead from the same period shows the BJJA as members of the WJJF with James Blundell 7th dan carrying the title Soke, and with Bob Clark and Ronnie Colwell (who was now training at the Lowlands) both listed as chief instructors and 5th dans.

This letterhead also lists Jack Holt (4th dan) as the 'Area Organiser Secretary North'. Jack Holt had also been developing his own Karate-based style of martial arts and was teaching in Accrington. This letterhead highlights that James Blundell's style, and the BJJA organisation, were becoming home to additional styles and clubs. One of Jack Holt's best students, Martin Dixon, would subsequently go on to become the future chairman of the BJJA(GB).

In conversations with BJJA(GB) historian David Brough I learnt that while growing up in Accrington Martin Dixon had found a Kempo Karate club led by Jack Holt and by age 16 was a black belt. However, the turning point in Martin's martial arts career came in 1968 as an 18 year old when he watched a demonstration of Jujutsu in Bolton involving James Blundell, Bob Clark, Charles Allmark, and Ronnie Colwell. Martin was amazed at what he had seen and from that point on travelled from Accrington to the Lowlands in Liverpool every Thursday to train. Kenneth (Kenny) Blundell, James's son, started learning Jujutsu at the Lowlands in 1957 when he was just 6 years old.

At this time an affiliation to the Juko Kai appeared to be important for Jujutsuka training in the UK as it provided accreditation and certification that was otherwise lacking.

Pictures from the Lowlands in the mid 1970s show that former senior students of Jack Britten, Jimmy Pape (Chester) and Fred Kelly, were visitors to the Lowlands and can be seen wearing the Juko Kai badge on their gi. Following Jack Britten's death in 1978, another of his senior students, Mick Walsh, also affiliated to the Juko Kai (in addition to the Chew Choo Soot affiliation mentioned above), but remained independent of the BJJA. At this time momentum was building around the BJJA and the style developed by James Blundell who now, along with Bob Clark, was developing some outstanding students, including Eric Marshall, Robert (Bobby) Ashworth, James (Jimmy) Pape (Liverpool), Paul Geoghegan, John Steadman, Charles Allmark, Paul Murray, Tommy Antrobus, Kenny Chisholm, Martin Dixon, and James's son and daughter, Kenny Blundell and Susan Allmark (nee Blundell). Another significant visitor to the Lowlands would be Richard (Dick) Morris from London.

Richard Morris was graded up to 4th dan in Aiki-Jujutsu by Alf Morgan. When Alf Morgan died Richard Morris arrived at the Lowlands eager to learn this dynamic new style being taught by James Blundell and Bob Clark. Morris also sent his student James McDade to the Lowlands to learn the syllabus. James McDade got his black belt in Aiki-Jujutsu with Morris in 1968. Bob Clark's students Eric Marshall and Charles Allmark travelled to London to teach Morris the syllabus. The scene was set for a major development and expansion of the style which was driven by Bob Clark.

The British Ju Jitsu Federation

Another Jujutsu association was developed post-WWII by Vernon Bell. Better known for helping establish Karate in the UK, Bell actually spent most of his time learning and teaching Jujutsu. Bell taught Jujutsu from around 1944 to his death on February 27th 2004 at the age of 81, and in addition to 60 years of teaching held the grade of 10th dan in *Tenshin* Shinyo Ryu, though it is almost certain that he never studied the Koryu version of Tenjin Shinyo Ryu.

Bell giving one of his famous demonstrations in the late 1950s with Michael Manning at Ilford Baths. [Picture courtesy of Mr Manning]

Vernon Bell was born on October 9th 1922 in Essex, where he lived for most if not all of his life. In 1939 he joined the RAF and was introduced to Judo/Jujutsu in 1941 by colleague Ray Keene, and soon began coaching the art. Bell left the RAF in 1946 and continued to practise Judo as well as weight training and body building. He joined the Health and Strength League and subsequently became a member of the Amateur Judo Association (AJA) under Pat Butler. Pat Butler had been a student of Gunji Koizumi at the Budokwai from age 15. In 1949, Bell became a full time professional Judo instructor, teaching in his garage. In 1950, it appears Bell gained a 1st dan in Jujutsu. According to Bell's account (in *Shotokan Dawn* by Clive Layton) Bell took his 1st dan Jujutsu with the Anglo Japanese Judo and Ju Jitsu Society based in Cape Town, South Africa. Bell apparently graded under Harry Johnston and Oliver Thorne and was taught by a Sieshi Teppi.

According to the records of Jonathan Kruger of the Kodokwan Judo Ju Jitsu club in Zambia, Johnston did indeed introduce Judo/Jujutsu to the area having trained under Teppi (the spelling of which varies, including Seishi Teppei). However, there is also a document that suggests Johnston taught a correspondence course. It is possible therefore that Bell in fact gained recognition under Johnston via a correspondence course. When asked of this possibility, one of Bell's longest serving students said this was a definite possibility and said he doubted Bell had gone over to Cape Town, and had indeed mentioned a correspondence course. According to Bell, his 1st dan was in Tenjin Shinyo Ryu, and Kruger confirms that Johnston at least claimed to teach this style.

In 1952, Bell took another 1st dan, this time in Judo under Pat Butler and Harry Ewen. He took his 2nd dan one year later and his 3rd dan under Kenshiro Abbe of the British Judo Council in 1958. In Jujutsu Bell apparently passed 2nd dan in 1955 under Harry Ewen again, in Ilford but through the 'Mombasa Ju Jitsu Association' which despite its exotic name was based in Leicester. In 1956 Bell established the British Ju Jitsu Federation (BJJF), a response to James Blundell's BJJA. Bell also travelled to Paris to learn Yoseikan Karate from Henry Plée (who incidentally was now a Judo student of Mikonosuke Kawaishi). In correspondence recorded in *Shotokan Dawn*, Bell wrote to his Karate teacher Henri Plée in 1957 explaining the state of British Judo/Jujutsu.

Bell remarked: *'six big associations that are disjointed and in a terrible state.'* Bell also bemoaned the issue of Judoka such as Ernest Harrison and Kenshiro Abbe claiming to teach Karate, an art they had apparently not formally studied.

Between 1956 and 1964 Bell fully submerged himself in promoting the art of Karate in the UK, establishing his British Karate Federation (BKF) in 1957, and is rightly considered the father of the British Karate movement. Affiliated first to Minoru Mochizuki's Yoseikan, and then to the Japan Karate Association's (JKA's) Shotokan, he tightly controlled British Karate, and aside from token efforts to teach Karate by Harrison and Abbe, there were very few British Karateka outside of his circle. Among the exceptions were Charles Mack in Japan and Martin Stott and Danny Connor in Manchester.

Michael Manning was one of Vernon Bell's senior students in the 1950s. At the time Bell would only teach Jujutsu to those already studying Judo, and then would only teach Karate to those already studying Jujutsu. Bell also had a rule that students had to join in pairs so they had someone to practise with. He was also renowned for charging in guineas, an older British unit of currency which the younger students in the 1960s would have found unusual. Michael Manning told me: *'Most people who knew Vernon Bell would agree that he was a most complex character. As a young callow, skinny lad I at first held him in awe, later my opinion changed to one of respect and affection. My Jujutsu experience moved between Judo techniques, various locks and atemi waza and even a short course of Aikido. I remember learning how to deal with a greased burglar (without the grease) and of course the famous Sumo neck twist. We were taught how to use rolled up magazines, fountain pens, metal combs and various methods now deemed as unlawful - all good stuff!'*

Bell breaking planks at an Ilford Baths demo.
[Picture courtesy of Michael Manning.]

Even by the standards of the 1960s, Bell was not very politically correct. In Dennis Martin's *Working with Warriors* there is an interesting quote from Karateka Terry O'Neill regarding events between Vernon Bell and the great Japanese Karateka Hirokazu Kanazawa when he first visited the UK: *'Bell bought fish and chips and said "You'll have to eat yours here because the wife doesn't like Japs or Chinks," and left him outside on the doorstep.'* While that is an interesting reflection on UK society from that time, it is fair to say that Vernon Bell was a fairly unusual character. Known to have an interest in the occult, Bell also found employment as a hypnotist.

Manning offers similar anecdotes. He told me: *'My time with Vernon was unique bearing in mind this was the mid 1950s even for that time he was the most non P.C. person I have known. During an Aikido course we were attending given by Tadashi Abe, direct pupil of O Sensei Morihei Ueshiba it was made known that Abe Sensei had been involved during WW2 with Kamikaze kaiten submarines, Vernon exclaimed quite loudly "He couldn't have been any good as he is still here." On another occasion Kenshiro Abbe was holding a Judo grading. My friend was being tested by way of Randori and Abe Sensei was bouncing him like a rubber ball, Vernon shouted to my friend, "Don't let him get to you George, remember the Burma Railway." Luckily Abe Sensei hadn't a great command of English especially as I was up next! One evening in order to add realism to his lesson Vernon pounced out on a lady pupil, she screamed and Vernon was hauled before the principal of the college. On top of this type of behaviour there were of course Vernon's Hypnotic adventures - enough for a book in itself!'*

Vernon Bell, centre, with his first ever Karate class in 1956. Michael Manning, who provided this picture, is to his immediate left. The others include Ken Elliot and Trevor Guillfoyle

The first city outside Essex or London where Bell was able to successfully promote Karate was Liverpool. Here he had a captive audience because Jujutsu/Judo were already popular. His early Karate students in Liverpool included Judoka Fred Gille, Andy Sherry who had trained to green belt in Jujutsu under Jack Britten, and Terry O'Neill whose father had trained under Gerald Skyner. However, around 1964 Bell began to lose his vice-like grip on British Karate. The monolithic organisations of Shotokan, Wado Ryu and Shotokai arrived and students naturally gravitated towards the athletic and physically dynamic young Japanese masters such as Hirokazu Kanazawa, Keinosuke Enoeda, and Sadashige Kato. Bell gradually faded into obscurity concentrating on his so-called Tenjin Shinyo Ryu Jujutsu.

105

One of Bell's senior students was Terry Wingrove. He is of significance because as well as being a senior student of Bell's he was also integral to the establishment of the International Ju Jitsu Federation (IJJF). Terry Wingrove was born in London in 1941 and claims that in 1952 he began training in Judo at the Budokwai. In 1957 Wingrove started Karate with Vernon Bell's Yoseikan, having already joined the Jujutsu club.

Michael Manning kicks Terry Wingrove during a
Vernon Bell organised demo circa 1960

In 1967 Wingrove arrived in Japan and became an officer with the Federation of All Japan Karate Organisations (FAJKO). During this time Wingrove also trained Jujutsu with Kimbei Sato, who taught many styles of Jujutsu including the Yawara system Yagyu Shingan Ryu. It was while living in Japan that Wingrove arranged for Bell's groups (the British Karate Federation, British Ju Jitsu Federation and European Ju Jitsu Union, which Bell had formed with Alfred Hasemeier) to be recognised by Masafumi Suzuki's Seibukan in Kyoto. The Seibukan run by Suzuki taught all forms of martial arts. It is thought that the marriage of the Seibukan with the EJJU led to the formation of the International Ju Jitsu Federation (IJJF) in 1968 between Suzuki, Alfred Hasemeier and Vernon Bell. In 1973 the Japanese Seibukan Academy recognised the IJJF as its world branch for Jujutsu and the EJJU as its branch for Jujutsu in Europe. In 1981 the IJJF apparently applied for UNESCO membership.

Kimbei Sato was born in 1925 in Fukushima and graduated from Tohoku University Department of Medicine with a Ph.D. in medicine, which helped in his understanding of the human body as it relates to martial arts. As well as mastering several styles of Jujutsu, he was also among the first Japanese masters to be a

106

recognised lineage holder in several Chinese martial arts. He became Chairman of the All Japan Chinese Martial Arts Federation, Honorary Chairman of the Beijing Ba Gua Zhang Research Society, Honorary Advisor to the Eastern Chi Gung Society (Beijing), and Advisor to the Beijing Martial Chi Gung Society.

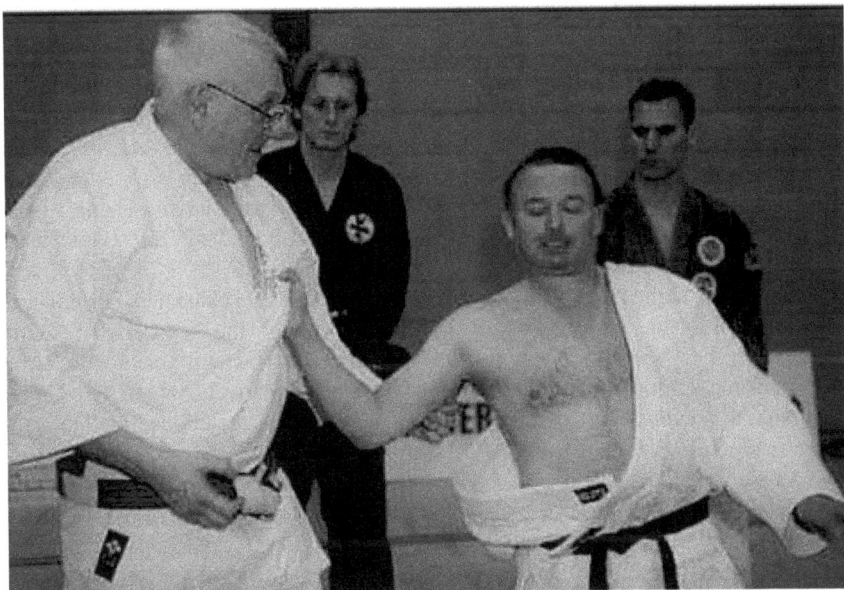

Terry Wingrove teaching a technique on a course in Wigan in 2006. Author Simon Keegan and Andy Manwaring seen in the background.

Sato began teaching police officers at Japan Police College in 1954 and opened up his own dojo in Itabashi, Tokyo in 1958. As well as the many traditional martial arts he mastered he also formulated a system based on his own clan traditions called Daiwa-Do.

Sato once said of his studies: *'I have expanded my studies from Jujustu, to Chinese martial arts, to qin na, to pressure points, to chi-gung, and finally to Taoism. Anybody can learn to combine the techniques of reversals, throws, locks, thrusts, and kicks. The integration of my Jujutsu with chi-na and other martial arts is slowly coming to fruition, and its completion as a method for bare-handed fighting or with weapons is near. Jujutsu and Chinese martial arts make up the path that I have pursued and that have guided my life.'* Another style Sato studied was Tenjin Shinyo Ryu, famously one of the main styles that influenced Judo. Sato's daughter recalls: *'My father learned from Miyamoto Hanzo, who gained his licence in the art after studying under Inoue Keitaro and Yoshida Chiharu; because the Iso family line came to an end, it was Miyamoto who became responsible for carrying on the style as the 5th generation lineage holder. My father also received teaching in the style from Ono Sokichi of Ooshu Iwanuma, who learned Jujutsu and bone-setting from Yoshida Chiharu. Also, Inoue Takeo,*

107

the grandson of Inoue Keitaro, asked for some instruction in the art from my father during World War II when he was evacuated to Sendai.'

Perhaps the style of Jujutsu most closely linked to Sato was the Yawara system Yagyu Shingan Ryu. Perhaps Sato's experience in Chinese martial arts gave him an advantage in learning this art which does appear to be derived from Chuan Fa. According to Sato, this style of Jujutsu was more deadly than any other. His daughter recalled: *'It was 1950 when my father Sato Kinbei received his licence to teach Yagyu Shingan Ryu, just after he returned from the war in China. According to him, Yagyu Shingan Ryu is different from other forms of Jujutsu in terms of its practicality on the field of battle and its unrivalled fierceness and ability to kill the enemy. It is said that the experienced practitioner can shatter an enemy arm with one blow.'* Sato began studying Hsing-I in 1959, studying with Wang Shu Jin for eight years. He also studied Taiji, Bagua and Baji Chuan. Sato studied Baji Chuan under Zhang Zhong.

Sato's name nowadays is often linked to those of Takamatsu Toshutsugu and Ueno Takashi, who are well known for being the teachers of Bujinkan headteacher Masaaki Hatsumi. Sato was actually Hatsumi's senior and studied Asayama Ichinden Ryu under Ueno. This was solely an atemi (striking) and gyakute (reversal) art. Sato found that many of the techniques in this art were already known to him from Daito Ryu. In 1955 he became the art's grandmaster. As well as Jujutsu, this art also includes reversals with the Jo and Tessen. Sato also learned Tenshin-ryu and Bokuden-ryu from Ueno, but it was a two way relationship and he too taught arts to Ueno. From Takamatsu, Sato learned Kukishin Ryu Bojutsu, Takagi Yo Shin-ryu Jujutsu and Gikan Ryu Koppo.

It may be said that Sato also helped to resurrect some dormant styles including Araki Shin-ryu Jujutsu, which his great grandfather had studied, and Itten Ryushin Tyuukai Ryu, which was an amalgamation art of three styles, Isshin-ryu (from Sakuma Katusuke), Ryushin Tyuukai-ryu (from Miura Yoshiemon), and Tenshin Shin Yo-ryu (from Iso Mataemon). Sato's daughter recalled: *'My father was living in Iwanuma around 1953-4, and learned the art from its beginning from Ono, later receiving the written transmissions of the art to become the second generation in its lineage.'*

Another student of Bell's was Alan Ruddock. Ruddock was born in Dublin, Ireland, in 1944. At the age of 13 Ruddock took up Judo with the Irish Judo Association under Seamus Kavanagh after being bullied. Despite training Judo until 1959 Ruddock never graded. At this time Ruddock began writing to Vernon Bell and attending some of his courses. As the only Irishman to do so, Ruddock was quickly snapped up by Bell as branch representative for Ireland. Because Ruddock was a low grade at the time, his was considered a study group.

The British Karate Federation records Ruddock's first grading in April 1961 in Upminster as follows. It is interesting to see the grades because at the time, in British Karate, only Vernon Bell and Michael Manning would have held higher grades than Terry Wingrove, who was at the time just a 3rd Kyu (brown belt):

J Alibone (6th Kyu)
K Goult (5th Kyu)
Brian Hammond (5th Kyu)
E Harris (5th Kyu)
S Morgan (5th Kyu)
Alan Ruddock (5th Kyu)
J Shepherd (5th Kyu)
E Tillet (5th Kyu)
D Williams (5th Kyu)
Bob Buckner (3rd Kyu)
Terry Wingrove (3rd Kyu)

I originally contacted Terry Wingrove to ask him some historical questions about Karate and Jujutsu. That was in 2005. Terry said to me: 'You must come and train with me. Bring your passport.' I said: 'Why, where are we training?' and he said 'Poland. Don't worry about it, it's all sorted.'

Prior to the flight we stayed in Luton. Everyone travelling over was to stay in a B&B. I was sharing a room with Alan Ruddock. I couldn't believe I was actually getting first hand anecdotes about Morihei Ueshiba from one of his students. Alan was so softly spoken you couldn't hear him from a few feet away. I remember we got onto talking about Nikkyo and I asked him if he'd seen a particularly nifty reversal that I knew. 'Ah well, O Sensei did Nikkyo slightly differently to most people today,' and Alan then proceeded to slap on an incredibly painful Nikkyo. Needless to say my reversal didn't work.

When we arrived in Gdansk Terry took centre stage. I had never seen him on the mat before. I was expecting a kind of Shotokan-Jujutsu-Aikido hybrid. Instead he was showing what I would describe as pressure points or Kyusho, except far more painful and vicious. He explained these applications were Karate Jutsu and Yawara. Grown men were literally screaming as their flesh was torn, they were being choked, their eyeballs were popping out. I'd never seen anything like it. My turn came to be his Uke and he must have demonstrated a hundred excruciating techniques on me. I subsequently hosted Terry in seminars around the North West and after about 12 years he began to moderate his style of teaching towards me. In the end we would meet in a coffee shop in Manchester and he would apply gentle pressure points on my fingers and hands to demonstrate principles. I would sit with a notepad quizzing him about Sato Kimbei's Yawara, the Karate Jutsu of Fujiwara and Fujimoto.

In the 1960s Bell was affiliated to the Yoseikan under Henri Plee, Hiroo Mochizuki and Tetsuji Murakami, and so Ruddock got to see Aikido at Murakami's demonstrations. Inspired, he found a copy of Koichi Tohei's book and began to teach himself basic Aikido. Ruddock's training in Aikido would continue, as we see in the next chapter.

One of Bell's loyal students was Paul Masters, who started training with Bell in 1966 and held chief instructor positions in both Karate and Jujutsu under Bell. Masters travelled to Japan to train Tenjin Shinyo Ryu with Kubota Toshihiro Shihanke, where he realised that what Bell had taught him was not authentic

Tenjin Shinyo Ryu. Writing in a post on e-Budo in 2006 Masters stated: *'I started my martial art career in 1966 with Vernon, first learning some Judo then moving on to Karate and Ju-jutsu. The style of Ju-jutsu Vernon told me I was learning was Tenjin Shinyo Ryu or Tenshin Shinyo Ryu as he sometimes termed it and whose founder was Iso Mataemon. At this time I trained with him every day, sometimes 2-3 times a day, both in Karate and Ju-jutsu. After several years we parted. We rekindled our relationship in the mid 90's when I undertook private lessons from him, sometimes twice a week, in what he again told me was Tenjin Shinyo Ryu. During this period he told me that I was to become his successor and head of the Tenjin Shinyo Ryu organisation for this country. I have a signed letter from him to this effect. By this time I had dedicated most of my life to teaching and training other students including my son in the martial arts, in what I thought was Tenjin Shinyo Ryu. Following this several things happened that started putting doubt in my mind that what Vernon professed to be Tenjin Shinyo Ryu was in fact a Goshin westernised style of Ju-jutsu. I questioned Vernon as to the validity of the system of the style of Ju-jutsu we were doing and he was still adamant that it was the true Tenjin Shinyo Ryu of Iso Mataemon. He told me he had learnt it from a Japanese gentleman by the name of Seishi Teppi while in the airforce and stationed in South Africa, but in my own heart I knew all was not correct. As yet I have not been able to trace any information on Seishi Teppi, but even if this was true and I do not doubt that it was, whatever the Japanese gentleman taught Vernon, it was not Tenjin Shinyo Ryu as neither the techniques nor syllabus resembled anything like what I now know as Tenjin Shinyo Ryu. I have to say we parted company and I held a feeling of animosity towards him. However, that was now something like 11 years ago and much has happened to me in my martial arts career. I have also had time to reflect on the whole situation and I now personally believe that Vernon sincerely felt he had been taught and was teaching Tenjin Shinyo Ryu because probably this is what he was incorrectly told and this probably goes for many others out there. But I ask, if you cannot prove your lineage and do not have the correct credentials, then please, please do not call it Tenjin Shinyo Ryu. As we put in our first post, there is only one Tenjin Shinyo Ryu. Regarding the late Mr. Bell, I do not now feel any animosity towards him and he should be remembered as the 'Father of British Karate' because this is fact and he relentlessly worked to establish the Karate movement for this country and seeing today how many people practice karate, he was surely successful and therefore must go down in history as a great man. I would like to finish this long discourse by saying my only teacher now is Kubota Toshihiro Shihanke and the only martial art that I practice and teach is Tenjin Shinyo Ryu. I am the only westerner to date to have been taught the Gokui techniques, these are the higher secretive techniques of our style. In fact in July last year while I was training in Japan Sensei taught me the Kuden and told me that I was his first student that he had ever taught Kuden to. The Kuden is the inner teaching of our Ryu and contains all the principles behind the 124 fighting katas of our style and this was the last thing his teacher the late Sakamoto Sensei taught him. Also in July last year my son Lee was awarded his Mokuroku. He is the first person to be awarded this transmission under the authority of the*

Tenyokai U.K. and this was recognised and ratified in Japan by Kubota Sensei, President of the Tenyokai Japan. I tell you this not to blow my own trumpet but to give you the facts as they are. If I am a quarter as successful as Mr. Vernon Bell in propagating Tenjin Shinyo Ryu as he was in karate then I will be truly satisfied.'

Paul Masters went on to become the first legitimate British holder of the Menkyo Kaiden in Tenjin Shinyo Ryu. Paul Masters' son, Lee Masters, is now also Menkyo Kaiden in Tenjin Shinyo Ryu.

It is worth noting here however that there were earlier examples of British involvement in Koryu Jujutsu. An early example of British involvement in Koryu Jujutsu in Japan was Quintin Chambers. Chambers started practising Judo in 1954 whilst he was serving in the Navy. Following this Chambers attended Cambridge University, where he became captain of the University Judo team. Chambers travelled to Japan in 1961, initially to tutor for a British diplomat's family, and practised Judo and Aikido. It was here that Chambers met American martial arts pioneer Donn F. Draeger who, in 1962, introduced him to Shimizu Takaji of Shindo Muso Ryu. In 1965 Draeger also helped Chambers study Tenshin Shinyo Katori Shinto Ryu with Otake Risuke. Chambers and Draeger travelled together to research other martial arts in Asia, which resulted in multiple publications including a joint project on Kukishin Ryu with Masaaki Hatsumi. Chambers was one of the first Westerners to train with Hatsumi. Mike Finn was another instructor who began studying Judo in the 1950s. Like Chambers, Finn became friends with Draeger and through him studied Muso Shinden Ryu, Shindo Muso Ryu and was exposed to Tenshin Shoden Katori Shinto Ryu. It should be pointed out that Muso Shinden Ryu is considered Iaido (sword work), Shindo Muso Ryu is considered Jodo (using the Jo staff), Katori Shinto Ryu is best known for its Kenjutsu (fencing), Kukishin Ryu is best known for its Bojutsu (using the Bo staff) and Ninjutsu - so none of these schools are particularly renowned as Jujutsu schools per se, but as with all Koryu bujutsu, they do include some of what would be considered Jujutsu.

Given Paul Masters had studied both Koryu Jujutsu with Tenjin Shinyo Ryu, and Gendai Budo with Vernon Bell, I asked him what he felt were the main differences between Koryu and Gendai Budo. Paul kindly replied with the following article:

'It is both an honour and privilege to be asked by Simon to give an opinion of the differences between gendai budo-modern martial way and kobudo-classical martial way with particular reference to Jujutsu. To realise this ambition my qualifications of holding a 6th dan in modern goshin Jujutsu and a menkyo kaiden-licence of full transmission in Tenjin Shinyo Ryu kobudo Jujutsu, stand me in good stead to do so.

'There are two common generic terms in kobudo ryugi that distinguishes itself from modern goshin Jujutsu, these being kuden and hiden. Kuden is the transmission of teaching by mouth to ear from teacher to student. It is the teaching of the spoken word handed down from generation to generation regarding the inner traditions, philosophies and martial tactics of the ryugi, some of which may be fundamental to applying a technique correctly and some of

111

which is hiden-secret transmission. It should be pointed out that these teachings rarely change from generation to generation. Below is an example of such subjects:

Ju go seiru - the soft can overcome the hard.
Kuzushi - off balancing
Tsukuri - the way of entering for the execution of a technique
Kake - the correct execution of the technique
Zenshin - the forward mind
Tsushin - the active mind
Zanshin - the remaining mind
Maai - to close the distance by stealth
Metsuki - the un-nerving use of the eyes during combat
Kobo ichi - attack and defence are one
Ki no atsukai - how to control the energy

'As previously mentioned these are just some of the examples of the rigo-principles that involve kuden. Then within this teaching come the omote-outer teaching and the ura-inner teaching. To the observer the omote teaching maybe obvious whereas the ura is not so, being hidden within the application of the technique. Also within the hiden-secret transmission come the esoteric components, involving the three elements of mandala-visualisation, mantra-sound and mudra hand seals. Most kobudo ryugi originated historically from esoteric beginnings and therefore contain some esoteric teaching background.

'To give a complete treatise on the subjects mentioned above would take a whole book. Therefore it is my aim and objective to highlight one or two particular principles that may fulfil the requirements for this subject.

Like many kobudo Jujutsu systems Tenjin Shinyo Ryu has many principles that one must adhere to, not only for the correct physical application of the technique but also more importantly the correct shin po-mind/heart method. In our ryugi we have a most important kata called shin no kurai. This kata is regarded as the mother form of all the 124 two man forms of our ryugi. Not only does this kata-form contain all of the five major kamae-postures but also in addition to this it transmits to the monjin-student many of the major principles, essential for the correct application of technique and mind-set.

For example, transmitted within the teaching of this kata are three heart/mind methods, known as zenshin-the forward mind, tsushin-the active mind and zanshin-the remaining mind. These three heart/mind methods transmit how the mind should be applied during the different phases of a fight. For example zenshin is the mind of readiness preparing oneself for the engagement of the teki-enemy.

This is the mind of showing aggression on the outside, a strong fighting spirit but remaining calm on the inside. It is the mind of setting your ki down to the tanden-the lower abdomen while giving the kake goe or kiai-spirit shout. Next is tsushin, this is the mind during the action of the fight, the explosive mind, a mind that out of calmness comes hakkei-explosive ki-energy. Then there is zanshin the mind that remains focused after the final stage of the combat, a mind that is clear

112

and alert ready to go again. Furthermore these three heart/mind methods put together form the principle known in our ryugi as "kobo ichi" attack and defence are one. Here lies a major difference from my experiences both in modern goshin Jujutsu and classical ancient Jujutsu. What is the meaning of kobo ichi?

Fundamentally kobo ichi teaches the martial art student to attack the enemy just before they are planning to attack you. It is therefore both counter-defensive and pre-emptive at the same time. When the enemy is intent on attacking you, attack first. This is kuzushi-breaking the enemy's balance, both his physical balance and his mental balance. By off balancing the enemy's mind-set allows you to control the enemy by maintaining the winning position, not allowing the enemy any advantage.

Within kobo ichi comes the principle "hito nage" "hito shime" "hito ate" hi satsu Jujutsu-one throw, one strangle, one strike certain death Jujutsu. The meaning of this concept is plain to see with the finishing of the conflict as quickly as possible. Mostly from my experience modern goshin Jujutsu systems rarely transmit these principles; training is mainly by go no sen-counter attack.

'After thirty odd years training in a gendai Jujutsu this transition was difficult at first to comprehend. Attack the enemy before they attack you, this principle was one of the first encountered in my tuition and training from Kubota Toshihiro my late sensei when he transmitted the kata shin no kurai to me. This kata teaches the requirements for how to apply kobo ichi. Again there are three principles, kuzushi, tsukuri and kake they are classical principles within our ryugi and are important when applying the principle of kobo ichi. Kuzushi as we have already explained is the off balancing of both your enemy's body and mind. Tsukuri is the way of entry in order to apply the technique and kake is the correct execution of the technique. To apply Kobo ichi we are taught that we must keep both the mind calm and the body relaxed, filling the body with ki-energy and to observe and become aware of the enemy's changes.

'From a personal point of view as a child, the neighbourhood that our family lived in was a tough environment. My memory of playing on the streets was very competitive and often would lead to fights even at this young age. One such memory was when around five years of age, being naïve in such matters finding waiting to be hit was the wrong approach, running up to my father for sympathy and consolation, only to get a slap far harder and told not to come crying again otherwise a harder slap would be coming. Little did I know at that time that some years down the line this would be a similar lesson introduced to me in Tenjin Shinyo Ryu Jujutsu.

'There is in the world of kobudo the saying "shin ken shobu"-real live blade, win or lose. In a real fight you either win or lose there is no second chance you either remain alive or you are killed. This teaching concept can easily relate to modern times with the increase of knife crime now on our streets. Fortunately this type of encounter has never happened to me. However one can never guarantee that this is never going to happen to you, nor can you predict the outcome of such an event. In such an altercation do you wait to be stabbed at? In reality the chances of parrying and disarming a frenzied attack are slim, but on many occasions this is what is transmitted in modern goshin Jujutsu systems, counter

113

defence. Why wait to be stabbed at in rapid fashion and by multiple thrusts of the knife. This mind set can cost you your life. The principle of kobo ichi-to pre-empt the attack, and maybe by using diverse tactics may save your life, by taking the initiative and controlling their knife hand rather than waiting to be stabbed. Kobo ichi and the principles contained within are in my opinion one of the major differences between gendai budo Jujutsu and kobudo Jujutsu. There will of course be some out there who will read this and disagree with me and this may spark some debate. From my experiences however observing and learning both systems old and new there is a major difference. This difference lies in the rigo-principles that are transmitted with the principle of kobo ichi being one of them that influences both the techniques and mind-set.'

It is worth reflecting on the broader importance of Vernon Bell and James Blundell's contributions to British Jujutsu. While Skyner and Britten had also sustained Jujutsu in the UK, they had done so as single style clubs. Bell and Blundell formed seemingly outwardly looking associations, the BJJF and the BJJA respectively, that broadened the promotion of their respective styles, and generated a home for other Jujutsuka. The individuals coming through the BJJF and BJJA would sow the seeds for the future development of Jujutsu in the UK. Bell and Blundell had provided the inspiration and the vision.

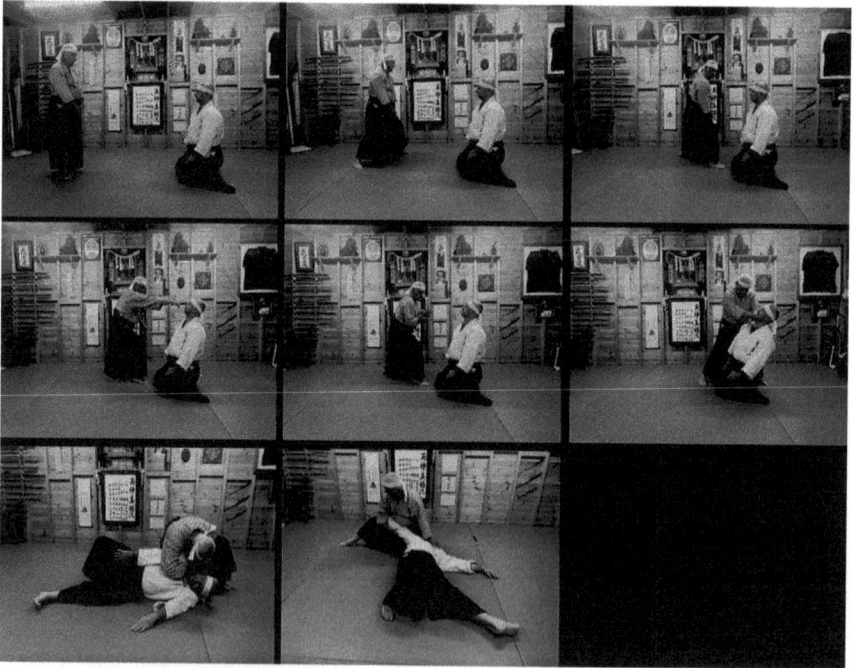

Paul and Lee Masters practising the shin no kurai kata

Kenshiro Abbe

It is important to spend a little time discussing one of Bell's teachers - Kenshiro Abbe. Kenshiro Abbe was born in 1915, on the island of Shikoku in the Tokushima Province. Abbe took up Judo aged 14, and at age 16 he became the youngest ever to achieve 3rd dan, which he received directly from Shohei Hamano of the DNBK. By 1938, aged just 22, Abbe was a 6th dan in Judo and considered to be one of the most formidable Judoka in Japan. Also in 1938 Abbe fought top Kodokan Judoka Masahiko Kimura, as well as three other high ranking Judoka in a contest. Abbe beat them all, including the great Kimura, who was heard to comment afterwards: *'It was like fighting a shadow.'* Kimura would famously defeat Helio Gracie in Brazil in 1949, breaking his arm with a gyaku-ude-garami which would become known as the 'Kimura'. In 1945 the DNBK awarded Abbe his 7th dan in Judo and 6th dan in Kendo.

Abbe also became a master of Aikido. The story of how he discovered Aikido is particularly interesting as recalled by Keith Morgan and Henry Ellis in a 2006 edition of *Martial Arts Illustrated*. It was when travelling on a train that Abbe noticed an older man staring at him. This old man subsequently asked Abbe if he was a 5th dan in Judo. Abbe replied: 'Why yes, how did you know that?' The old man replied: 'Because you have the build of a 5th dan. So who are you?' Abbe replied: 'Everyone knows who I am, I am Kenshiro Abbe, Judo champion of all Japan!' The dialogue between Abbe and the old man continued until the old man put his finger in Abbe's face and said: 'You are so powerful, break my finger!' Abbe grabbed the finger expecting to snap it, except he suddenly found himself on the floor. Amazed at the old man's skill Abbe asked who he was. The old man replied: 'I am Morihei Ueshiba, the founder of Aikido.' Abbe immediately asked Ueshiba if he would teach him Aikido, and subsequently studied with Ueshiba for the next 10 years. It is interesting to note that the moral of the tale in which Abbe meets Ueshiba is repeated throughout martial arts, as we see with the tale published in the *Idler* discussed in chapter 4. Martial arts enable the smaller/weaker/older/more humble to overcome the stronger champion.

In 1955, now age 40, Abbe travelled to the UK to train at the London Judo Society. In 1958 he formed the British Judo Council with Masutaro Otani. Abbe established a reputation as an exceptional Judoka. At a training course with Abbe, Vernon Bell's student Michael Manning remembers an occasion when a student thought they could get the better of Abbe. Manning told me in a letter: *'During a lesson I was waiting for my turn to train with the great man (Abbe), a well built American 1st kyu remarked to me "He's an old man, I reckon I could take him." During a lull I approached Abbe Sensei and told him the American would like randori with him. Abbe Sensei agreed but at the time was keeping an eye on a group of juniors practising on another mat. With children and beginners he was most gentle and understanding, however not so with this stupid 1st kyu. The brown belt kept attacking with Okuri-Ashi-Barai (leg sweep), Abbe Sensei being short and very solid the American couldn't break his opponent's balance and just kept bruising his leg. As this technique was one of Abbe Sensei's favourite throws he became rather miffed at the brown belt's lack of skill. He then went more or less through the Nage-no-kata. The poor bugger didn't know what had hit him! Just to add insult to injury Abbe Sensei continued to tutor the kids whilst hammering his opponent into the mat. When it came to my turn I was bounced but not in a vicious way, it was in fact an honour. This was just one of many sessions with the great man, very talented and very humble.'*

In addition to Bell, Abbe would influence many Jujutsu instructors, although Abbe himself was technically a Judo and Aikido practitioner. His students included several Jujutsu pioneers. Two students of Abbe's that must be viewed as notable Jujutsu pioneers were Norman Grundy of Scarborough and Kevin Murphy of Birmingham. Grundy had apparently begun his training under William Garrud and may have even trained under Sadakuza Uyenishi. Grundy, along with wealthy ice cream magnate Peter Jaconelli, opened the 'Ippon Judo Club and Institute of Budo' on Huntress Row, Scarborough in 1959, where it remained until 1968 when it relocated to the former Technical College on Valley Road. The club hosted many notable instructors such as Abbe, and Vernon Bell's BKF held its annual 'summer school' there with Tetsuji Murakami. In 1970 the club moved again to the Old Church, Seamer Road, Scarborough and continued for another 10 years until the club relocated for the last time to the Castle Hotel until 1983 when the hotel burnt down. By 1974 Grundy had achieved the grade of 7th dan.

Kevin Murphy moved from Birmingham to Scarborough in the mid-seventies where he established the Budokan Club. In 1983 Murphy would relocate his club to the former premises of the Ippon Judo Club and Institute of Budo in the Old Church, Seamer Road. Also in 1983 the European faction of Kokusai Budoin IMAF headed by Minoru Mochizuku became an autonomous federation. Mochizuki held many high grades including 10th dan Aikido, 9th dan Nihon Jujutsu, 8th dan Iaido and 8th dan Judo, and was responsible for the development of IMAF in Europe and the UK. Mochizuki held the rank of 9th dan in Nihon Jujutsu based on his studies of Daito Ryu and Gyokushin Ryu. The Nihon Jujutsu division was later taken over by Shizuya Sato, a student of Kenji Tomiki. Mochizuki awarded Kevin Murphy the grade of 7th dan Kyoshi in Judo and Nihon-den Jujutsu – the first Englishman to receive the award. Kevin Murphy went on to become the UK Director of the Kokusai Budoin IMAF. When Murphy left IMAF he was succeeded as UK Director by one of his early Birmingham students Dave Wareing (6th dan Judo), and as UK Secretary by one of his Scarborough students Colin Hutchinson (6th dan Judo), who had also trained with Grundy.

Another notable student of Abbe with connections to IMAF is Jack Hearn of Cramlington, near Newcastle. Hearn began Judo in 1951, and was graded up to 4th dan by Abbe. Hearn became a senior technical advisor to Kokusai Budoin in 2004 when at the time he held the rank of 8th dan in both Judo and Nihon Jujutsu.

Two of Abbe's students in Germany may have been Judoka named Wolfe and Hassermayer. Wolfe and Hassermayer are noted as the instructors of Mathew Komp who emigrated to Melbourne in 1953 and started teaching Judo and

Jujutsu. One of Komp's students was Brian Graham who had earlier emigrated to Australia from the UK and who had returned to the UK in the 1960s. Graham was now practising a style of Jujutsu that he had named Shorinji Kan Jiu Jitsu. One of Graham's first students was Peter Farrar, who helped expand the style to form an organisation called the National Samurai Jiu Jitsu Association (NSJJA). In 1990 the NSJJA became The Jitsu Foundation (TJF) and has a strong presence in British universities.

Other students of Abbe's included Gordon and John Warfield. At a course in Wales in 1963 Gordon and John were awarded 1st dan by Abbe. With the help of Abbe they would form Goshinkwai Jujutsu which would later become a member of Rod Sacharnoski's Juko Kai. A notable student of Gordon and John Warfield is Dave Turton, who would go on to form the Self Defence Foundation and the All Styles Martial Arts Association.

IMAF course circa 2003 including, front row: First left author Simon Keegan (at the time 2nd Dan Nihon Jujutsu), next left: John Lovatt (Muso Jikiden Eishin Ryu and Nihon Jujutsu), next left Dave Wareing (Judo, student of Kevin Murphy), centre Colin Hutchinson (Judo student of Kevin Murphy). Second from right: Ray Walker (Judoka). Back row includes Reiner Parsons and sons Derrick, Graham and Clive, Goju Ryu Karate practitioners.

Another Jujutsu practitioner who may have originated in the Kenshiro Abbe line was Brian Dossett, later a 10th dan and 'soke' of his own system, Spirit Combat. Dossett, who boxed and studied Judo as a youngster, also training in the merchant navy, studied Aikido under Ken and David Williams, under the auspices of Abbe. In an interview with *Martial News*, Dossett explained his early training as follows: *'I started boxing at the Isleworth Boxing cub back in the late 40s aged nine years old and then Judo when I was 12 years old. During my teens I joined a Karate club and later continued in with Sensei Abbey [Note, here he probably means Kenshiro Abbe], Nakazono [unknown] and Harada [almost*

certainly Shotokai Karateka Mitsusuke Harada who was associated with Abbe]
including Aikido and wrestling.' Dossett was considered controversial in the
1970s for things that would be considered tame today (wearing a blue gi, teaching
an eclectic Western system and so on). Dossett was considered a 'wind up
merchant' and once performed a weapons kata with a garden fork wrapped in
tinsel. According to one of his students, this was only because a lawn mower
wouldn't fit in the back of his car! As well as his controversial stunts, Dossett
was renowned for 'putting his money where his mouth was' and even as an older
man took part in full contact fights. He had one spirited fight against freestyle
Karateka Dicker Hopkins that was covered in *Martial Arts Illustrated*, and
showed that even as an older man, Dossett did indeed have the boxing skills he
claimed.

Author Simon Keegan with Naginata one of the 18 arts

Among Dossett's students to break away from Spirit Combat were his cousin
George Scarrott and Jaimie Lee-Barron. Scarrott and Lee-Barron founded their

own Jujutsu system in around 1993 called Kiai Yamabushi Ryu. I graded 2nd dan in this system in 2001 and recall that it included some 18 martial arts (Bugei Ju Hapan) which were: 1) Koppo Jutsu, 2) Koshi Jutsu, 3) Karate Jutsu, 4) Atemi Jutsu, 5) Aikijutsu, 6) Ju Tai Jutsu, 7) Bo Jutsu, 8) Jo Jutsu, 9) Iai Jutsu, 10) Kenjutsu, 11) Tanto, 12) Jujutsu, 13) So Jutsu/Naginata Jutsu 14) Gunryaku Hei ho Jutsu, 15) Inton, 16) Gotonpo, 17) Tenchijin, 18) Kusari Jutsu.

As a side note one of Abbe's other students would also have an impact on UK society. Peter Thornley started training with Abbe as a teenager and achieved his black belt before a finger injury curtailed his Judo aspirations. However, Abbe had a profound influence on the young Thornley and inspired the wrestling persona Kendo Nagasaki that was adopted by Thornley, and who would thrill British wrestling fans for decades. Abbe would spend his final years back in Japan and in poor health. In 1985 Abbe suffered a stroke, and subsequently died a month later.

Alan Ruddock was also continuing his journey in Aikido. As a merchant navy radio officer, Ruddock travelled all over the world, including to Japan, where he visited the Aikido headquarters in Tokyo, the Aikikai Honbu Dojo, to view a class. Morihei Ueshiba wasn't present on that occasion; however, Ruddock did meet Henry Kono and Ken Cottier who would later help him obtain a Japanese visa. Ruddock returned to Ireland and took a week long summer course in Aikido run by Kenshiro Abbe's student Ken Williams in England.

Ruddock told *Irish Fighter Magazine* of his return to Japan in 1966: *'Morihei Ueshiba was the real reason for my Aikido pilgrimage to Japan. I had read quite a bit about this miraculous old man and having seen the pictures – I wanted the real thing. I knew what he did was special and wanted to be like that too – but I did not feel the same "Wow – this is something else!" kind of response that others report. I was impressed and intrigued – but not overawed. My journey to Japan was a personal spiritual quest and I realised that this man was someone you only get to be around once – he was a true mystic. Over the coming months and years I was to see him on a daily basis (when he was in Tokyo). As a karate man with both judo and jujitsu experience, I was not easily impressed by people flying through the air for apparently no reason. I had made a huge effort by modern standards to be there to learn what was on offer but – over the first few months I began to think – "Can this really be true, these guys are just falling over..." Then, little by little, as other guys who had 'gone for him' described their bewildering experiences of falling ('for no good reason') and also my own careful observations of the reactions of his uke's – I was convinced that this man was incredible.'*

Ruddock trained every day of the week at the Aikikai Honbu Dojo, where, during this time, Ruddock was the only Irishman, and Ken Cottier was the only Englishman (though Terry Wingrove was also there briefly) training under Ueshiba. Ruddock graded up to 4th dan with the Aikikai and subsequently up to 6th dan with the DNBK.

The Rise of the BJJA and the WJJF

In the mid 1970s martial arts in the UK were required to have a 'governing body' in order to access funding from the Sports Council. In 1976 James Blundell's BJJA reconstituted itself as the governing body and, along with the governing bodies of other martial arts, was invited by the Sports Council to form the Martial Arts Commission (MAC). Events leading to the new BJJA coincided with Bob Clark forming a new World Ju Jitsu Federation (WJJF), to which the BJJA would remain closely associated. Richard Morris was now the Chairman of the BJJA, and the Director of the WJJF, and Bob Clark was Chief Instructor to both and the WJJF International Co-ordinator. Giacomo Bertoletti of Milan would become the WJJF International President. James Shortt was invited to be the Secretary of the new BJJA. Beryl Miao was the WJJF Company Secretary.

Bob Clark launched the new WJJF from new headquarters at Barlows Lane in Fazakerley in Liverpool with students previously of the Lowlands. Clark's vision was to take his brand of Jujutsu global. In the early years there was still some alignment with Sacharnoski's Juko Kai organisation. An early international association was with the French Jujutsuka Roland Maroteaux, who was teaching a blend of Hakko Ryu Jujutsu, a derivative of Daito Ryu, and Aikido, a form of Aiki Jujutsu which he termed 'Goshin Do'. The picture which was to become the badge of the WJJF was actually of Roland Maroteaux throwing student Alain Sailly.

A student of Maroteaux from this time was Kirby Watson. Kirby Watson's martial arts career started in 1973 in Karate under Terry O'Neill and Cliff Hepburn at Salford University, where he would become a member of the University team which went on to win the British Universities Championships. In 1977 Kirby moved to France, where he met Maroteaux and was introduced to Goshin Do. He received his black belt in this art in 1979 under the WJJF affiliation, shortly before returning to live in Britain. Kirby would remain on the periphery of the BJJA/WJJF, running a club in Perth, Scotland until 1984. When Kirby left the BJJA/WJJF he continued to study Hakko Ryu Jujutsu with Roy Hobbs, an American Air Force Colonel who was stationed near Ipswich at the time, and with Antonio Garcia from Belgium, eventually achieving 4th dan in 1989. Since 1985 Kirby's main style, which he currently practises and teaches, has been Kaze Arashi Ryu under US based teacher Henri Robert Vilaire.

Further documentation from this time demonstrates how quickly things were moving. The BJJA licence book issued in 1975 showed Rod Sacharnoski as Soke of the WJJF, and James Blundell as International Co-ordinator, Chairman of the BJJA, and a 7th dan. In a licence book issued in 1978, a mere 3 years later, Sacharnoski (10th dan) and Blundell (now Soke and 9th dan) were patrons, and Bob Clark was 8th dan and President and International Co-ordinator. A dan grade certificate issued in early 1979 shows the Juko Kai association.

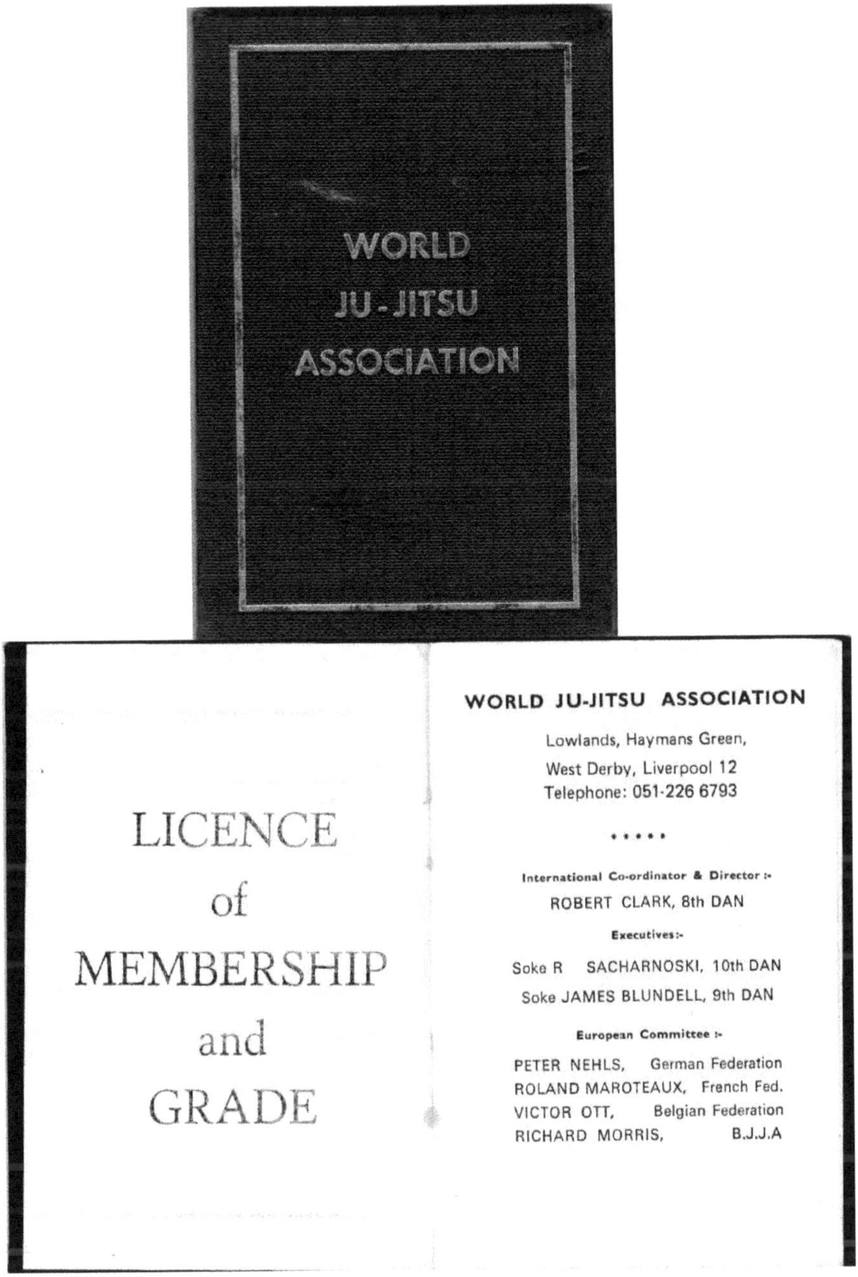

WORLD
JU-JITSU
ASSOCIATION
LICENCE
of
MEMBERSHIP
and
GRADE
WORLD JU-JITSU ASSOCIATION
Lowlands, Haymans Green,
West Derby, Liverpool 12
Telephone: 051-226 6793
International Co-ordinator & Director :-
ROBERT CLARK, 8th DAN
Executives:-
Soke R SACHARNOSKI, 10th DAN
Soke JAMES BLUNDELL, 9th DAN
European Committee :-
PETER NEHLS, German Federation
ROLAND MAROTEAUX, French Fed.
VICTOR OTT, Belgian Federation
RICHARD MORRIS, B.J.J.A

License book issued in 1978 showing Bob Clark as 8th Dan and Jim Blundell as 9th Dan. Pic, courtesy of Kirby Watson

Shodan certificate issued in 1979 to Kirby Watson. It was shortly after this that certificates were rebranded with the new WJJF logo described above.

In July 1979 a coach carrying the cream of the BJJA/WJJF left the Lowlands and travelled to Sicily for an international event to celebrate the formal beginning of the WJJF. These were heady times for the WJJF. Jujutsu was enjoying a massive increase in popularity and there was a sense of great excitement and adventure from those involved. The course in Sicily brought together associations from many other countries under the WJJF banner. There would be two training sessions per day; the first at 7am in the morning and the second between 6-7pm in the evening. Certificates commemorating the event were handed out at the end.

Top panel, the team assemble at the Lowlands in Liverpool before departing to Sicily, July 1979. Bottom panel, on the coach, front left is Bob Clark, behind him is Jimmy Pape (Liverpool), and to the left of Jimmy is Kenny Blundell. [Pictures provided by Eric Marshall, BKR Jujitsu]

Top panel shows Spartaco Bertoletti and Richard Morris signing certificates in Sicily, July 1979. Bottom panel shows Eric Marshall demonstrating an arm lock and a kick. [Pictures provided by Eric Marshall, BKR Jujitsu]

There was real momentum now behind the WJJF. In September 1979 the WJJF published a training manual with Bob Clark demonstrating the WJJF syllabus and featuring Eric Marshall as the main uke. By now Clark was managing clubs in the north and Morris managing clubs in the south. Accounts from students training at the time suggest that the WJJF syllabus was a modified and enhanced version of the BJJA syllabus developed by James Blundell, which was in turn, it would seem, developed from Raku Uyenishi's books.

BJJA/WJJF demonstration team picture taken at the Lowlands in May 1978.
[Picture provided by Eric Marshall, BKR Jujitsu]

The massive rise in popularity of the BJJA/WJJF was principally due to two reasons. The first was the strong influence of the BJJA and the MAC over Jujutsu in the UK. The second was due to the demonstration teams that travelled all over the UK and Europe putting on Jujutsu demonstrations. Both factors driving the popularity were masterminded by Bob Clark. Before long Clark and the demonstration team were in great demand, such was their formidable reputation. The members of the demonstration team were the cream of the BJJA/WJJF, each an outstanding martial artist. With every demonstration new clubs were formed or signed up to the WJJF. According to the *World Ju Jitsu Federation Program Training Manual* by 1979 there were associations in 44 countries that had signed up to the WJJF programme. The demonstrations combined elements of several different aspects of Jujutsu, and were fast paced and dynamic; and they were funny, with the Liverpool humour and banter contributing to the spectacle. It is also worth noting here that the demonstration contained a routine based on

Vigny's la canne, in which Eric Marshall would fight with Kenny Blundell using an umbrella to defend himself. Eric Marshall had first learned walking stick techniques in the 1960s at his first club under the instruction of Bert Roberts.

Such was the growth of the BJJA/WJJF that senior instructors were now running their own clubs on a regional level. Eric Marshall was now running clubs in and around Liverpool. John Brunskill, who earlier had been a student of the Chester Jimmy Pape, had moved to Liverpool in the late 1970s and had become a student of Eric's. John gave an account of being a student of Eric: *'Back in the 1980s Eric had a dojo in Crawfords social club in Wavertree. I think it was open at least 2 evenings in the week and Sunday morning. There were 2 mats, the old-fashioned type of canvas stretched over foam rubber with a wooden frame. Anyone who has ever trained on this type of mat will well remember the smell, and of course the pain inflicted if your ankle hit the wooden frame! Eric was always keen on proper mat etiquette, bowing on and off the mat. You could only address Eric as Sensei or Mr Marshal and definitely no shoes on the mat, ever! So I'm training one Sunday morning, I guess I'm a blue or purple belt, and we are practicing escapes from a side head chancery, the one when you are being pulled along. I have my partner by the neck and he performs his escape, which is a variation on a valley drop throw, and I land on my back. Unfortunately my partner's fist ends up between my back and the mat. The pain was unbearable and much to Eric's disgust, I'm screaming the place down (pain was to be endured in silence). To be fair Eric quickly realised it might be serious and called an ambulance. While waiting for the ambulance to arrive, training continued on the other mat and I was left in the middle of the mat because I'm in too much pain to be moved. The ambulance arrives in due course and the medics come into the hall just as one of the other students takes a punch to the nose, no doubt distracted by the arrival of the ambulance! In any event the ambulance crew go straight to assist the chap with the bloody nose, ignoring me in the process. Well Eric loses it, not because they went to the wrong casualty, but that they dared to walk on the mat in their shoes! Eric makes the ambulance crew take off their shoes before they put me on a stretcher, then put me down at the edge of the mat to put their shoes back on!'* John Brunskill would subsequently open a club in Banbury, Oxfordshire, in 1992 under Eric before retiring to South Africa in 2006, since when he has run the Blue Crane Bujitsu Ryu.

In addition to the Liverpool centric instructors, other instructors were also expanding. Martin Dixon covered the Accrington and Blackburn area. Robert Ashworth had clubs in Skipton, Colne and at Burnley. Robert Ashworth had started training in Karate in Skipton in the late 1960s. Two things then happened. The Karate club would close and Robert would see a Jujutsu demonstration by members of the Lowlands. He was so taken with the demonstration that he then started travelling to the Lowlands to learn Jujutsu and subsequently established a Jujutsu club in Skipton as part of the BJJA. Robert would travel to the Lowlands where James Blundell had son Kenny teach Robert the white belt and then yellow belt syllabus. James Blundell then gave Robert the syllabus sheets for white and yellow belt and encouraged him to teach what he had learnt back in Skipton. This would continue with Robert travelling to Liverpool to learn the whole syllabus from James Blundell and Robert Clark. John Idle started with Robert Ashworth in 1978 in Skipton and achieved his 1st dan in 1981. Richard Asbery started training with Robert Ashworth in 1976. On the 10th of December 1983, the same day John Idle took his 2nd dan grading, 15-year-old Richard Asbery took his 1st dan at the Lowlands where James Blundell, Bob Clark, and Kenny Blundell were the grading panel.

As the BJJA/WJJF continued to expand, so did the individual instructor clubs, with Robert Ashworth soon running additional clubs in Barnoldswick, Nelson, Padiham, Lancaster, Blackpool, Halifax, York, Bradford, and Preston. John Idle recalled the expansion of Robert Ashworth's clubs: *'This gave the more dedicated students many training options and it was not unusual to attend all of them in any given week.'*

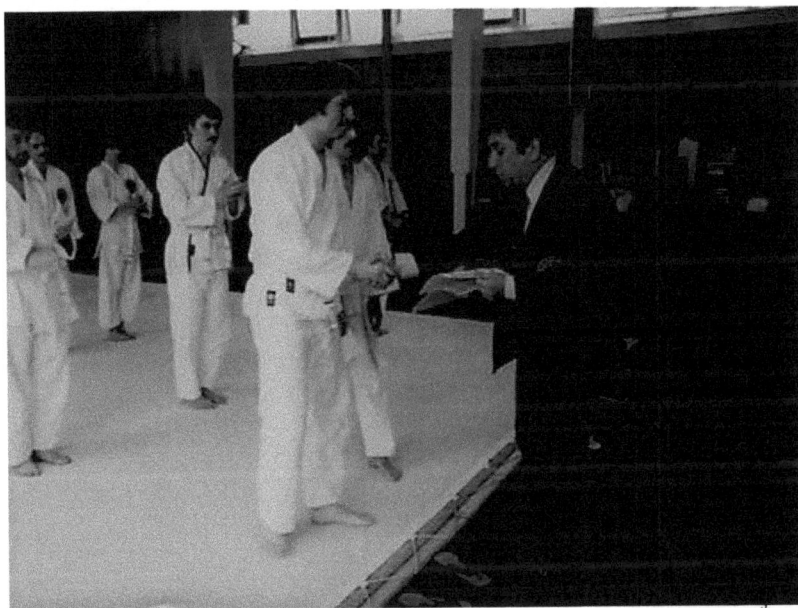

Picture of Bob Clark awarding Chris Henry his white belt on March 7th 1982 at Mereside. [Picture provided by Chris Henry of the Bushido Ju Jitsu Academy, BJJA(GB)]

Other core members of the BJJA/WJJF team included Jimmy Pape. An article written by BJJA(GB) historian David Brough published on the Knutsford Bushido website gives some insight into Jimmy. Jimmy was born in 1944 in Liverpool and had started Jujutsu in his mid twenties. Jimmy was no stranger to confrontation and knew how to handle himself working as a doorman in the pubs and clubs of Liverpool.

It was after a visit to the Lowlands, where he was watched a young Paul Geoghegan and Robert Ashworth throwing each other around, that Jimmy started Jujutsu. Jimmy didn't need Jujitsu as he had already developed considerable

127

skills from working the doors in Liverpool and from being in the merchant navy. In the merchant navy Jimmy had worked down the coast of South America. Jimmy recalled falling out with a fellow Scouser when his ship was docked in the Port of Santos in Brazil: *'This fella said you don't like me do you, and I said nah, and so we went ashore to have it out. There was a big square surrounded by bars, and everyone came out to watch the fight. Must have been a thousand people watched that fight and I let him have it. However, half an hour after the fight he knocked me out with a bottle over the back of my head.'* Jimmy's determination to win meant he never lost a fight. However, he could see what extra advantages and skills he could add to his armoury by learning Jujitsu. Jimmy's first and main instructor was Bob Clark. As Jimmy was working as a doorman he was able to train with Clark regularly during the day. Jimmy's black belt grading panel was James Blundell, Bob Clark, and Fred Kelly. Kenny Blundell, son of James Blundell, was already a junior black belt before Jimmy started, and was also a dedicated Jujutsuka. John Steadman was already training in Karate when he started training in Jujutsu at the Lowlands.

Paul Geoghegan's first instructor Frank Garner teaching at an Aikido course in Leeds on the 23rd November 1969.
[Picture provided by Tony Underwood, BJC]

Paul Geoghegan started martial arts aged 10 when he took up Judo at Frank Garner's Ko Bu Kan Judo Club within the AJA at Childwell Lane, Liverpool. In addition to Judo Frank Garner also taught Karate, Kendo, and Aikido. Training under Frank Garner (then a 3rd dan in Judo), Paul Geoghegan achieved black belt in Judo.

Charlie Allmark had been practising Jujutsu at the Lowlands under James Blundell since the age of 10, and while working together with Paul Geoghegan, both serving apprenticeships as sheet metal workers, suggested that he come to the Lowlands to give it a try.

At age 17 Paul Geoghegan walked into the Lowlands for the first time and didn't look back. Frank Garner would subsequently take his Ku Bu Kan Judo clubs into the BJC in 1978 when he was ranked 4th dan, and five years later into IMAF. Paul Geoghegan didn't practise Judo again, or ever speak to Frank Garner, but his training in Judo was to have a profound influence on how he practised Jujutsu. Paul Geoghegan was determined to be the best he could at Jujutsu and trained as frequently as he could.

By 1975 Paul had achieved black belt. On his grading panel for 1st dan were James Blundell, Bob Clark, Charlie Allmark, Eric Marshall and Kenny Blundell. Taking their black belts on the same day were Robert Ashworth and Tommy Antrobus.

From the mid-1970s onwards Paul Geoghegan was Bob Clark's main uke and travelled all over the UK and Europe delivering demonstrations and courses. By the mid-1980s Paul had established several clubs, notably in Chester, Ellesmere Port, and in Plas Madoc, Wrexham, which he would collectively call the Bushido Ju-Jitsu Association.

This group, Jimmy Pape, Paul Geoghegan, Kenny Blundell, Eric Marshall, John Steadman, Robert Ashworth, and Charles Allmark, amongst several others (Paul Murray, Tommy Antrobus, Kenny Chisholm) under Bob Clark became core BJJA/WJJF instructors and stalwarts of the demonstration team. In terms of talent this was a golden era for the BJJA/WJJF.

Another Jujutsuka of note was Allan Tattersall, who began training with James Blundell and Bob Clark around 1965. Tattersall attained the rank of 2nd dan with the BJJA and achieved 4th dan with the BJJA/WJJF. In 1983 Tattersall also began Iaido with Okimitsu Fujii of Muso Jikiden Eishin Ryu. Tattersall once remarked that studying Iaido *'clashed with the policy of the WJJF'*, which would ultimately result in his departure. Fujii introduced Tattersall to his teacher Haruna Matsuo, master of Muso Jikiden Eishin Ryu. Haruna Matsuo was the chief instructor of the Musashi dojo in Okayama and apparently one of only eight men who also taught Niten Ichi Ryu, the double sword art of Musashi. Tattersall claimed: *'My life changed really dramatically during this period.'* Haruna even invited Tattersall to his home in Japan in 1986.

The action was not exclusively northern however. Richard Morris was now controlling the south for the BJJA/WJJF. James McDade was Morris's most senior student and was running the adult classes at Morris's London Ju-Jitsu Centre in the 1970s before establishing his own Meadway Jujutsu clubs in 1979/1980 in the areas of Tottenham, London, and Barnet, Hertfordshire. James

McDade achieved 5th dan in 1982 and 6th dan 1988 with the BJJA/WJJF, and served as a committee member of the BJJA until 1991. James McDade's son Stephen passed his black belt at the London Ju-Jitsu Centre in 1983 aged 16.

Picture of some of the prominent BJJA/WJJF Instructors taken in the mid 1980s. Back row left to right are Paul Geoghegan, Jimmy Pape, Eric Marshall. Front row left to right are Robert Ashworth, Charles Allmark, Kenny Blundell.
[Picture provided by Eric Marshall, BKR Jujitsu]

Another noticeable early recruit to the organisation was Terry Parker. Terry Parker's first introduction to Jujutsu was as a young man in a police station, when trying to join the London Police Cadets. Writing in his autobiography *The Full Circle* Terry states: *'We the candidates were taken to Snow Hill Police Station canteen for lunch and I suppose I looked bored because some kind constable gave me a book on Ju-Jitsu by the famous Yukio Tani. I read and absorbed its every word and felt an immediate affinity with the art.'* Terry didn't get into the police and ended up doing his national service in the army, where he practised some boxing, Judo, and some other martial arts while posted to Korea and during a visit to Japan. Upon leaving the army Terry started training in Judo, in which he achieved a black belt. After searching for a Jujutsu instructor he found Vernon Bell. From *The Full Circle* Terry states: *'At last I found a Master in the area (Essex), a man I admire greatly to this day. His name is famous for being the first man to bring Karate to Great Britain, Dr. Vernon Bell.'* Regarding Vernon Bell Terry stated: *'I have been taught by many people, but no one has ever been able to best him as far as I am concerned.'* Terry was soon running his own club within Bell's Federation. Things came to a head however when he tried to establish another club. The BJJA was now the governing body with the Martial Arts Commission, and so joining the BJJA, and subsequently the WJJF, was important for legitimacy. Thus Terry Parker left Bell's organisation and joined the BJJA/WJJF. Soon Terry, with the help of his wife Janet, was running many clubs within the BJJA south and had called his group the Jikishin Ju Jitsu Association.

Another important development by Bob Clark to the BJJA/WJJF dan grade syllabus was the introduction of Okinawan Kobudo. John Idle recalled the introduction of Okinawan Kobudo: *'This widened the students' general portfolio, but some felt it departed from our core unarmed Jujutsu work. Weapons training proved to be a key tool in enabling large and otherwise unwieldy class sizes to be manageable.'* Bob Clark would run training seminars on Okinawan Kobudo and would award certificates of competence. One such certificate awarded to John Idle is issued from the 'Society of Okinawan Ko-Budo'.

High points of the BJJA/WJJF era were visits to the UK by senior Japanese Jujutsuka. In 1984 Soke Inoue travelled to the UK, where joint seminars between Hontai Yoshin Ryu and the WJJF were conducted. John Idle attended one of the seminars put on in Rochdale with Soke Inoue and his son Kyoichi Munenori (who is now the current and 19th Soke). Other notable attendees at this course included Jimmy Pape, Bob Clark, John Steadman, Allan Tattersall, and Eric Marshall.

The WJJF had grown rapidly and soon many of the senior instructors started to leave and establish their own organisations.

In 1987 Allan Tattersall and Robert Ashworth both left the BJJA/WJJF and subsequently established a Jujutsu federation called the United Kingdom Jujitsu Association (UKJJA, later UKJJAI (I=International)). John Idle had graded to 3rd dan within the BJJA/WJJF and now found himself within the UKJJA where he would take his 4th dan. Under the tuition of Tattersall John would also study Iaido. In 1987 John bought an Iaito (sword) from Tattersall which was one of two presented to him by Haruna Sensei during one of his trips to Japan.

In 1986 Richard Morris resigned from his positions in the BJJA and WJJF and left the organisations to found a new organisation called Jiu Jitsu International. In 1991 Morris also co-founded the World Kobudo Federation with John Therien and Alain Sailly. With more than 60 years training in Jujutsu Richard Morris achieved the rank of 10th dan. On the 15th July 2019 Richard Morris passed away aged 83.

The BJJA and the WJJF would part company. Martin Dixon, who had graded to 6th dan with the BJJA/WJJF, took the reins of the BJJA. In 1988 a new BJJA was reconstituted led by Martin Dixon. Martin established the Masters of Martial Arts (MMA) organisation to run his clubs in and around Accrington and taught a style of Jujutsu called Goshin Kempo, based on the syllabus taught by James Blundell.

Certificate from the Soke Inoue course in Rochdale in 1984 provided by John Idle of the Bushido Ju Jitsu Academy, BJJA(GB)

In the late 1980s James Blundell had been in failing health. Already frail from a previous stroke, on the 13th November 1989 James passed away after suffering another stroke. After James's death Kenny Blundell took the Lowlands Ju Jitsu Association out of the WJJF. In an eulogy for his father Kenny wrote: *'the messages of condolence at his funeral came from near and far, in respect of a man who was a pioneer of Jujutsu in the country.'* Few could disagree that James Blundell had been one of the great pioneers of British Jujutsu.

In 1987 Eric Marshall also resigned from the WJJF. Eric then established his Bugei-Ki-Ryu (BKR) Jujutsu clubs, which he would subsequently take into the newly reconstituted BJJA. In 1990 John Steadman left the WJJF and formed Ronin Yudansha Ryu.

The last of the golden generation to leave the WJJF were Paul Geoghegan, Jimmy Pape, and Charlie Allmark. In 1991 Paul Geoghegan, Jimmy Pape, Charles Allmark, Eric Marshall, John Steadman, and Kenny Blundell, and their constituent clubs, joined forces to form a new association called the Bushido Ju Jitsu Academy under the auspices of the BJJA.

Picture from a Bushido course in November 1991 in Sutton.
[Picture provided by Eric Marshall, BKR Jujitsu]

Terry Parker also resigned from the WJJF and took his Jikishin clubs into the newly reconstituted BJJA. Ian Arbon started as a student of Terry Parker in 1985 and remembers grading to 2nd dan in 1990 shortly before Terry split with WJJF.

James McDade remained within the BJJA/WJJF until 1991, when he and his son Stephen decided to take their Meadway clubs private, affiliating now with the Amateur Martial Arts Association (AMA). In 2003 James McDade established his current organisation, Total Self Defence, where he is now 10th dan, with son Stephen now 8th dan.

Another student of Vernon Bell's students who taught Jujutsu and Karate was Mike Newton of Leigh. Mike Newton had begun his training in Judo and then became a practitioner of Yoseikan Karate and Jujutsu under Trevor Jones with Vernon Bell's British Karate Federation.

As a result of Terry Wingrove's contacts in Japan, Bell's group became affiliated to Masafumi Suzuki's Seibukan and Newton took his 2nd dan under Suzuki. Suzuki had trained with Chew Choo Soot, and Newton subsequently made contact and a Budokan instructor came to Britain. A year or so later, Chew invited Newton to Kuala Lumpur to train with him. There Newton was not only taught Karate, but also the double broadswords and Double Dragon stick (a Shaolin based bo form). Newton trained in Kuala Lumpur for three months and a year later Chew himself came to Britain.

Shotokan instructor Phil Handyside (who had taken his black belt under Hirokazu Kanazawa but begun his training in Judo and Jujitsu in 1963 under Richard Butterworth) received an invite from Chew to escort him around the

North West to promote Budokan Karate and was awarded his 2nd dan. Handyside organised the KBI World Open Championships in 1979 at the Preston Guild Hall. At this point Newton and Handyside were both 2nd dan in Budokan Karate; both, having started Karate in approximately 1966 (and Judo/Jujutsu three years earlier), had at least 12 years' training. Newton was voted President of Karate Budokan Great Britain with Handyside as Vice President. According to an interview in *Fighters* magazine in 1984, Newton was graded 4th dan at the time and ran a club called the Bushido Dojo. In 2003 Newton, who already held 7th dan in Budokan Karate, was awarded 7th dan in Yoseikan Karate, 7th dan Kobudo and 7th dan in Jujutsu by Bell. Newton was the first Karate/Jujutsu instructor of my first formal sensei, Steve Bullough.

Handyside, who began in Jujutsu in 1963, studied martial arts for 55 years before he was awarded the grade of 9th dan in Karate. Although primarily a Karate instructor, Handyside was known for his Jujutsu locks and throws and dynamic demonstrations with the katana. I was awarded 5th Dan and 6th Dan by Mr Handyside.

The author with Phil Handyside in 2012

The Martial Arts Commission and New Federations

On the 3rd July 1990 the leaders of the major Jujutsu groups within the UK got together with the Martial Arts Commission (MAC) and the Sports Council for a meeting at the Kingsley Hotel, Bloomsbury Way, London. The purpose of the meeting was to establish a new governing body to represent the interests of everyone practising Jujutsu in the UK. The Sports Council, with input from the MAC, subsequently chose to recognise the BJJA as the governing body, which in 1993 became called the BJJA(GB). The new BJJA(GB) was to be, in Martin Dixon's words: *'A broad church, not dictated by any one style.'* The original AGM of the new BJJA(GB) took place in 1996 at the Roman Way Hotel, Watling St, Cannock.

Picture of the original BJJA(GB) executive committee from 1996 provided by Martin Dixon. Front Row, left to right: Sheila Dixon (secretary), Eric Marshall, Tom Hibbert, Kevin Moore (Sport England Representative and development officer), Martin Dixon (Chairman), John Steadman, Alan Jenkinson (Treasurer). Back Row, left to right: Steve Allison (Vice Chairman), Mike Mclure, Paul Lloyd Davies, Mike Player, Jimmy Pape

Coinciding with the re-establishment of the BJJA(GB) was the establishment of a new international Jujutsu organisation. In 1991 several leading Jujutsu instructors formed the United Nations of Ju Jitsu (UNJJ). The UNJJ was established as a non-profit organisation to promote friendship and Jujutsu. From the UK Martin Dixon, Jimmy Pape, and Terry and Janet Parker were amongst the founding members, and it was Martin Dixon who designed the UNJJ badge. Within the first year of the UNJJ it was registered in Belgium by Royal Decree and in the name of the King of Belgians, and signed by the Ministry of Justice. The UNJJ now hosts a biannual course and competition for member state associations (of which the BJJA(GB) is one) at a different location around the world on each occasion.

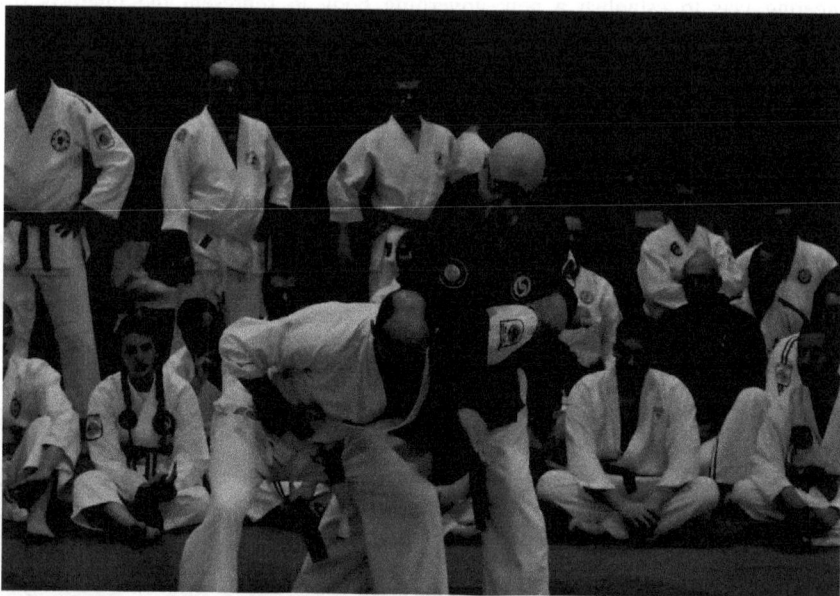

Picture of Jimmy Pape teaching at the UNJJ course in Gibraltar in 2018. Uke is Phil Rhodes of the Bushido Ju-Jitsu Academy.
[Picture provided by Andy Walker of the Bushido Ju-Jitsu Academy, BJJA(GB)]

While the BJJA(GB) was reinventing itself, so too was the WJJF. Bob Clark rebuilt and rebranded the WJJF. Now Alan Campbell replaced Paul Geoghegan as Bob Clark's main uke and became instrumental in the running of the WJJF. In 1992 Robert (Bob) Hart started training at Alan Campbell's club in Southport and stayed there for about 12 months before moving to Tony Young and Gary Forster's club in Skelmersdale.

During this period there were also changes within the UKJJA. Robert Ashworth found himself ousted as UKJJA treasurer by Tattersall.

Robert Ashworth subsequently left the UKJJA in around 1992. At this time John Idle, and others, were looking for a new direction, and John, his friend and training partner Norman Hudson, and his wife Barbara, set up West Craven Ju-Jitsu club in 1995. They were soon joined by Richard Asbery and Philip Atkinson who were also long-time BJJA/WJJF and UKJJAI students. In 1997 John recalled seeing an advert in the magazine *Fighters*: *'The Bushido Ju Jitsu Academy were advertising themselves as an organisation run for love not money and "free from politics." Their leadership read as a who's who of the Liverpool "golden*

136

generation" with Charles Allmark, Eric Marshall, Paul Geoghegan, Kenny Blundell and Jimmy Pape named. I got in touch with Jimmy and we were welcomed with open arms.' John, Norman Hudson, Richard Asbery and Philip Atkinson bought a property in Earby, Lancashire, in 2000, and officially opened the customised dojo for Bushido Barnoldswick in 2002 with James Pape and Paul Geoghegan as guests of honour. Bushido would then suffer splits with Eric Marshall taking his BKR Ju Jitsu out of Bushido and the BJJA(GB). John Steadman then did likewise with Ronin Yudansha Ryu. Kenneth Blundell left Bushido but remained part of the BJJA(GB). Charles Allmark passed away in 2000 leaving Jimmy Pape and Paul Geoghegan to lead Bushido. Robert Ashworth continued with his own organisation, RA Defence, until he temporarily retired from martial arts in 2008. In 2018, Robert Ashworth returned to Jujutsu as a member of the Bushido Ju Jitsu Academy and the BJJA(GB).

[Bushido Barnoldswick dojo opening. In front are John Idle and Jimmy
Pape. Back row left to right are Norman Hudson, Richard Asbery, Philip
Atkinson, Paul Geoghegan.
[Picture provided by John Idle of the Bushido Ju Jitsu Academy, BJJA(GB)]

During this period Allan Tattersall would strengthen his links to Japan. Tattersall would host courses with Japanese masters of Muso Jikiden Eishen Ryu such as the legendary Haruna Sensei, who was 28 times all Japan Iaido champion.

Tattersall would later tell a story about Haruna which shows the sense of humour of his teacher: *'One day in '99 we were sitting in his front room, when sensei asked me for my iaito. He took the fittings apart on the handle, asked Trevor to pass him a tsuba from a cabinet, fitted it on, then produced a new sageo and put that on. He then gave a little grunt and passed the iaito back to me in a* beautiful silk bag. Trevor sat open mouthed the whole time, then said "Haruna sensei has just put a 400 year old tsuba on your iaito."... I looked at him, then looked at Haruna sensei, then back at Trevor and keeping a straight face throughout the whole time I said to Trevor "ask him why he keeps giving me all his Old Stuff." Trevor nearly fell off his chair saying "I can't say that!" "Go on" I said, "ask him." After Trevor did, Haruna sensei looked with a stern face, stroked his chin, then burst out laughing. I did the same thing when I once asked him to translate a very old sake cup. At that time there were a couple of older sensei with us, each one looked at the Kanji then said "HaAAAA! a sake cup from the Kamikaze." "Oh." I said to Haruna, "sensei" I said, "Why did they wear crash helmets?" Same effect of stroking the chin, then a big laugh! That was Haruna. He once asked me when I was teaching "Tattersall-san! You say a different word when technique wrong." "Oh sensei, when?" He said "I say 'dame', what do you say?" "Oh I get it sensei, I use Crap!" "Oh good word, Yes! Sensei number one in UK" and sensei wrote it in his book. The next day on the seminar, Brian Bettison was doing a kata not to sensei's liking after showing him the points a couple of times. He exclaimed "Bettison-san Crap!" The whole room fell about laughing in tears! Haruna sensei looked at me in a stern manner and said "they laugh?" Quick as a flash I said "Yes sensei! They know now that you know the number one word in UK." "Hmmm!" he said.'

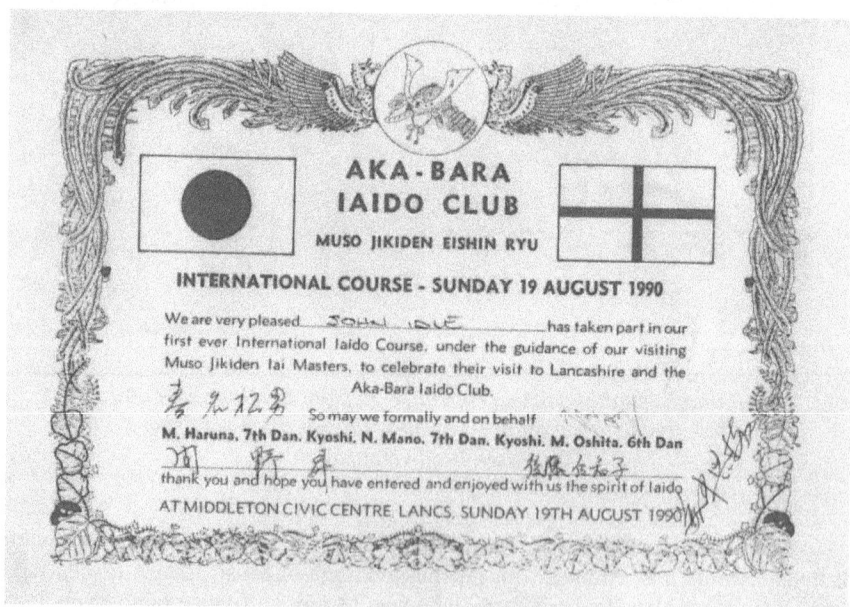

Example of a course in Muso Jikiden Eishin Ryu organised by Allan Tattersall and attended by John Idle.
[Picture provided by John Idle of the Bushido Ju Jitsu Academy, BJJA(GB)]

In Japan in 1992 the DNBK headquarters established an International Division, overseen by Tesshin Hamada. This succeeded the establishment of a DNBK division in the US in 1985. In 1995 Allan Tattersall was training in Takenouchi Ryu, said to be Japan's oldest pure Jujutsu style, founded in 1525. Tattersall was invited to join the Dai Nippon Butoku Kai and upon doing so was awarded 7th dan Kyoshi. Five years later Tattersall was awarded 8th dan. Then, in Japan, he was awarded the title Hanshi and was granted the position of Soke of his own ryu. He said: *'On the World Taikai in Kyoto after demonstrating again in front of 25 Hanshi, I was awarded the highest honour from Dai Nippon Butoku Kai in Jujitsu of Hanshi, and my style of Jujitsu designated as a new Ryu – Myo Shin Ryu Jujitsu! Meaning: Bright with the essence of true technique.'* In 2000, the first UK Butoku Sai (martial arts festival) was conducted in Manchester, England, coordinated by Allan Tattersall, where many Budoka from several nations joined in the coveted DNBK event. In 2003 John Idle earned his 1st dan in Iaido through Myo Shin Ryu.

I met Tattersall in 2006 at a seminar in Wigan. Following this I trained with him at his dojo in Rochdale and hosted him on seminars in Scarborough. Tattersall recognised the United Kingdom Budo Federation with 'shogo' titles and my father and I were awarded Renshi. I was admitted into DNBK under Tattersall's school the Myo Shin Ryu.

I'd met Allan Tattersall on a Terry Wingrove course and been impressed by his Iaido and Jujutsu – which I would say resembled Aikijujutsu more than anything. Fortunately my job took me to Rochdale in 2007, around the corner from Tattersall's dojo, so I would take my gi with me and train with him in my lunch hour. Like Terry he never charged me once for a lesson or seminar. Normally I'd turn up to chaos: his dog would be barking, his wife would be shouting at the dog and Allan would appear in a cloud of cigarette smoke. He'd normally say, 'Come in love!' (in that way older gentlemen from Rochdale call other men 'love'). We'd sit in his office and he'd show me tapes of him in Japan, magazines and his awards. It was like a museum. I'd ask 'Can we do some training Sensei?' and he'd say, 'Oh you wouldn't like that son.' And the next thing you know he'd be torturing me with some wristlock choke combo he'd learnt in the Takenouchi Ryu. Every time I left the dojo I'd come away with a gift, normally for my dad. Allan and my dad had trained in slightly different branches of Muso Jikiden Eishin Ryu and used to talk for hours about it. Allan would say something funny like, 'How's your dad son? Give him this hakama, tell him it's from Japan. It's not, it's from Pakistan, but tell him it's from Japan!'

Another Jujutsu student to work with Tattersall was notable Judo and wrestling competitor Trevor Roberts. Roberts, of Bolton, began his martial arts training in 1959 with Judo at the age of 9, and at 12 started freestyle wrestling, in which he became a British champion for his age group. Roberts then studied Jujutsu with instructors named Ross Nicholas, Jack Haydon and Norman Matthews, achieving 1st dan. Roberts was asked to teach at Jack McKeown's club, which Roberts says was 'ahead of its time' as it combined Jujutsu with boxing and catch wrestling.

A 1989 UKJJA leaflet lists Terry Wingrove (7ᵗʰ Dan), Robert Ashworth (6ᵗʰ Dan), Allan Tattersall (5ᵗʰ Dan) as the UK's senior grades. T Roberts, presumably Trevor, is also listed.

He was promoted to 3rd dan by John 'Nobby' Clarke, who was the first president of the UK branch of the International Budo Federation (IBF). Nobby Clarke's son Martin, and grandson John, would subsequently serve as presidents of the IBF. Roberts was awarded his 4th dan by Allan Tattersall and Dave Stretton, and 5th dan by Peter Schoneville of the IBF. Roberts was later promoted to 6th dan by the IBF in both shiai (combat) and traditional Jujutsu and made an IBF technical advisor. He would later be awarded 10th dan by Dave Turton. Among the students of Trevor Roberts is 'Meanstreets' instructor Russell Jarmesty, with whom I established *Martial Arts Guardian* magazine.

Outside large organisations such as the BJJA(GB), the UKJJAI, and the WJJF, other Jujutsu clubs were also developing. As discussed above, Mick Walsh, student of Jack Britten, had left the Alpha Ju Jitsu Institute and had established the Budokan Ju Jitsu Club after Jack Britten's death. Dave Williams started training with Mick Walsh in 1996 at his club in St. Hilda's Hunts Cross, Liverpool. In 2004 Mick Walsh passed away and Dave continues to run the Budokan Ju Jitsu Club from Hale Village, Liverpool.

Students from an UKJJAI course top. Course instructors in the bottom panel.
Course was held at Everton Sports Centre, Liverpool, 1991. Front, left to right:
Dave Stretton, Kirby Watson, Robert Ashworth, Alan Ruddock, Trevor Roberts,
Allan Tattersall, Danny Buckley, Leon Jay, Samuel Kwok.
[Pictures provided by Kirby Watson].

Former Britten students Frank Beatty and Billy Johnson were also still training. With Frank Beatty's support Billy Johnson established the Aiki Shin club in Liverpool with his wife Pauline. In 1996, former Eric George and Ken Cottier Aikido student Lee Hallard joined Aiki Shin. In Jan 2006, not long before his 82nd birthday, Frank Beatty contracted pneumonia in hospital and died. Up until that point he had been active on the mat. The Amateur Martial Arts Association (AMA) awarded Frank Beatty a 10th dan posthumously. Billy Johnson and Lee Hallard continue to run the Aiki Shin club.

In September 2003 WJJF National Coach Alan Campbell moved to Australia after the death of WJJF Australia representative Jan De Jong and established WJJF Australia. Bob Clark would now mentor a series of new ukes with a view to their potential leadership of the organisation. Bob Clark would run senior dan grade classes at Barlows Lane on Tuesday mornings and from 2004 Bob Hart, along with training partner Russ Walsh, would be in regular attendance. Bob Hart loved these sessions with Bob Clark and stated: *'Mr Clark never personally graded me, he usually only watched over all gradings. However, we would train on Tuesdays with him for 4/5/6 and 7th dan grades. He was a very tough teacher, took no prisoners, no matter what grade you were. He would scream at you regarding your body or foot position, and if he demonstrated on you then the contact was full on. He pushed you to your limit, then beyond if possible.'*

Mick Walsh and Dave Williams of the Budokan Ju-Jitsu Club. This picture is from 20th December 2001 when Dave Williams was promoted to 2nd kyu (at the time of writing Dave Williams was 3rd dan)

In October 2011 Bob Clark was overseeing the 7th dan grading of Gary Forster. Bob Hart was an uke this day and remembered that rather than the usual three people on the grading panel, this time it consisted of about ten of the most senior grades. At this grading Bob Clark made a statement to the senior grades about taking responsibility and about the organisation going forward. At this time it was clear to those who knew him that Bob Clark was unwell. In February 2012 Bob Clark passed away. It is fair to say that the organisation was not prepared for his death. In the uncertain period following Bob Clark's death it was Bob Hart, an accomplished businessman, who stepped in to establish a board of directors and convert the organisation to a Community Interest Company (CIC), where it is now owned by the members. Towards the end of 2018, following a course in Northern Ireland organised by Stephen Black, and attended by senior representatives of both the BJJA(GB) and the WJJF, it was announced that Alan Campbell was to become the Australia representative of the United Nations of Ju Jitsu (UNJJ) from the 1st January 2019.

Robert (Bob) Hart the Chairman of the WJJF.
[Picture provided with permission by Bob Hart, WJJF]

Further changes were occurring within the BJJA(GB). In 2002 Terry Parker stepped back from running his Jikishin organisation. Now a senior dan grade with Terry, Ian Arbon was ready to establish his own association. Ian Arbon stated: *'Terry spoke with Martin Dixon to maintain BJJA(GB) membership for my new organisation. On February 8th 2004 I resigned from Jikishin and Wakarashin Jujitsu was born.'* Other senior Parker students followed suit with Mark and Claire Fitzgerald forming Kokora Kai. Another large grouping led by Brian Mallon called the Stanford Warriors would also form in 2000. These three organisations remain within the BJJA(GB). The BJJA(GB) has continued to grow, with notable additions such as The Jitsu Foundation and the British Armed Forces Jiu Jitsu becoming member organisations. John Rake's East Midlands Ju-Jitsu Association (EMJJA) and Mick Holden's Mind Body Spirit organisations also joined the BJJA(GB), where they remain. Mick Holden was appointed as the Head of BJJA(GB) Anti-Doping, and is responsible for delivering Anti-Doping Workshops on behalf of the BJJA(GB).

Left: Picture of the Kokora Kai instructors Mark and Claire Fitzgerald and son Harry with Janet and Terry Parker at a course in Belgium 2003. Picture provided by Mark Fitzgerald; Right: Picture of Stanford Warriors instructors Brian and Scott Mallon with Terry Parker in 2011. [Picture provided by Scott Mallon]

The Blundell legacy at the Lowlands Ju-Jitsu club continues. Kenny Blundell is now assisted by son Wayne Blundell, who is the senior club instructor and a 3rd dan.

Under Jimmy Pape and Paul Geoghegan the Bushido Ju Jitsu Academy (BJJA(GB)) would also see further growth. During this period Jimmy Pape was also laying the framework for future coaches within the BJJA(GB) by working with Sport England to develop the coaching course. Jimmy Pape students included Dave Bushell (5th dan), Mark Wood (now 8th Dan UKBF), and Andy Smith (3rd dan). Jimmy handed the Wilmslow club to Dave Bushell, who subsequently passed it to Andy Smith in 2006. In 2017 Paul Geoghegan opened a customised dojo in Ellesmere Port called Bushido Ju Jitsu Academy Headquarters and installed his senior student Phil Rhodes (6th dan) as the chief instructor. On the 1st December 2018 the Headquarters gained Centre of Excellence status from the BJJA(GB).

Bushido Ju Jitsu Academy instructors David Brough, Phil Rhodes, and Andy Smith.
[Picture provided by Phil Rhodes]

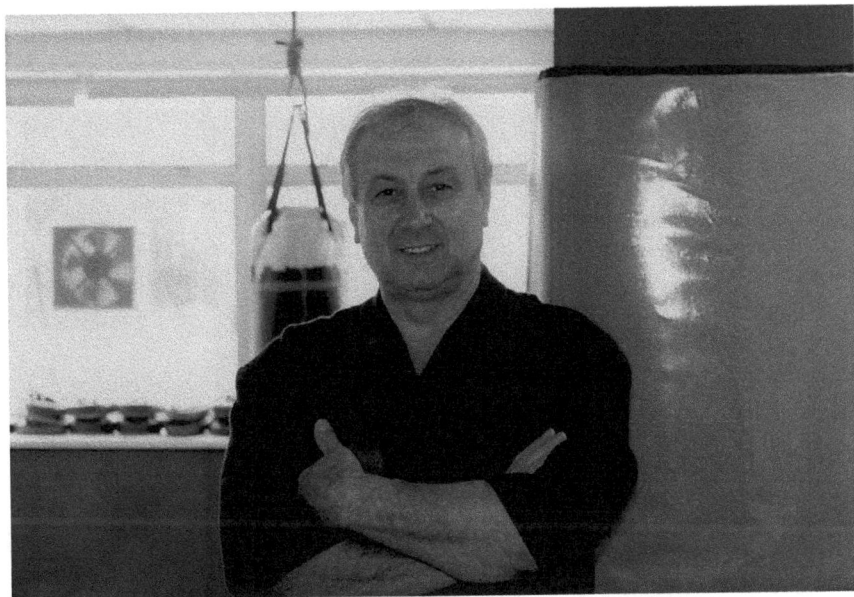

*Paul Geoghegan pictured at the Bushido Ju-Jitsu Academy
Headquarters in Ellesmere Port, 2018.*
[Picture provided by Andy Walker of the Bushido Ju Jitsu Academy, BJJA(GB)]

In his sixties Jimmy Pape was beginning to suffer from pains in his shoulders and neck and so he underwent an operation to resolve the problem. Unfortunately the operation went badly and for a period Jimmy was paralysed. This was devastating for Jimmy. Jimmy loved Jujitsu and being on the mat and this had been taken away. The pain was not just physical; there was considerable mental anguish, and it was his friends, particularly Paul Geoghegan, that kept him going. Jimmy had a six inch titanium plate put in the back of his neck and was told that if it was knocked he would be paralysed and thus couldn't go on the mat again. However, anyone who thought Jimmy was finished was wrong.

Ian Arbon, Chief Instructor of Wakarishin Jujitsu, said of Jimmy: *'In the many years I have known Jimmy, he has been a driving force in my Jujitsu. Not only is he a great master, he is also a great friend.'* Martin Dixon, the Chairperson of the BJJA(GB), who has known Jimmy for over 40 years, and had this to say about Jimmy: *'If I were to describe Jimmy Pape it would be "What you see is what you get". By this I mean, what you see is an awesome looking character, and what you get in times of need is an awesome character. Im proud to be his friend and colleague, and grateful that I am not his enemy.'*

Towards the end of Allan Tattersall's life the UKJJAI was in terminal decline, with many struggling to get along with him. Kirby Watson remembers receiving a phone call from Tattersall in 2014. 'Kirby', started Tattersall, 'do you know how many students I have now in the UK?' Kirby gave what he thought was a conservative estimate of several hundred. 'None!' Tattersall replied, 'they've all left me. They love me abroad though.' Allan Tattersall passed away on Tuesday the 18th of July 2017.

Allan Tattersall talking to David Keegan, at a UKBF course in Wigan in 2006

Things were also changing in Kokusai Budoin (IMAF). As mentioned above, Kevin Murphy was succeeded as UK Director by Dave Wareing and as UK Secretary by Colin Hutchinson. In 2005 there was a schism in the UK's IMAF directors, with Wareing retaining control of IMAF UK and Colin Hutchinson and myself running IMAF GB. A third branch, Kokusai Budoin UK, was established under Chris Davies. With the blessing of the late chief director Shizuya Sato, IMAF GB was established in 2005. IMAF GB would then become known as the UK Budo Federation (UKBF) with affiliated dojos in Scarborough, Manchester, Liverpool, Sheffield, Peterborough and Wigan.

In 2006 I held a masters course celebrating 50 years of British Karate and the British Ju Jitsu Federation, attended by Terry Wingrove, Allan Tattersall, Jack Hearn, Ronnie Colwell, Alan Ruddock and Tony Christian amongst others, to launch the UKBF, previously IMAF GB, of which I am still a director. In 2009 the UKBF became independent.

In 2018 I resurrected the UKBF with co-directors Mark Wood and Julian Mallalieu. Within the UKBF Mark Wood is the technical director for Jujutsu, and holds the grade of 8th Dan.

UKBF Masters Course 2006, from left Jack Hearn 9th Dan (IMAF), Allan Tattersall 9th Dan (Dai Nippon Butokukai), Tony Christian 9th Dan (Goju Ryu Karate, BKA), Alan Ruddock 6th Dan (Dai Nippon Butokukai), Terry Wingrove 9th Dan (IJJF)

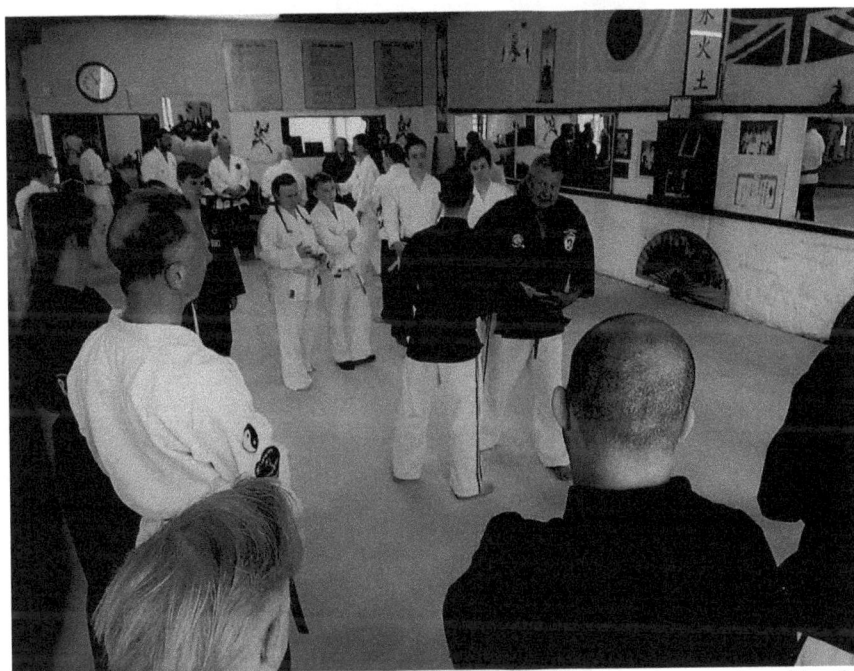

Andrew McConville 8th Dan teaching at Batley Budo, a course sanctioned by the UKBF.

Mark Wood started practising Judo in 1973 and trained until 1981, when he joined the WJJF training under Mark Kemp. In 1994 Mark took his 2nd dan with the WJJF and then left to join Bushido under Jimmy Pape. Mark stayed with Bushido until 2002, when he received his 4th dan. Mark recalled his time in Bushido: *'I absolutely loved my time in Bushido and Jimmy Pape is the best Jujitsu man I've trained with.'* Mark Wood also stated that Jimmy had helped him, and had pushed him, to develop his own direction, and had been a massive influence. This aspect of Jimmy Pape's mentorship was also echoed by Dave Bushell who graded to 5th dan with Jimmy and who said: *'Jimmy gave me the tools and told me to develop my own way.'*

UKBF Technical Director for Jujutsu Mark Wood.

Sport Jujutsu and MMA

In 1899 the DNBK formulated the rules for Jujutsu contests, and these were subsequently adopted by the Kodokan in 1900. Although it is clear Jigoro Kano did not intend Judo to become a sport, by 1964 it was an Olympic event. As discussed above, the early Jujutsu practitioners in the UK such as Tani and Uyenishi would compete against Catch wrestlers, and so, as stated, British Jujutsu was competitive from the outset. Catch wrestling would also continue to develop as a sport and it is worthwhile to chart a couple of these developments as they are relevant to our story.

Catch wrestling was the Western art most similar to Jujutsu. Hugh Leonard, an authority on the art, said in 1905 of a Jujutsu demo by Katsukama Higashi that he had been unable to find anything in Jujutsu which is not known by Western wrestling.

Even President Theodore Roosevelt studied Jujutsu, having previously wrestled and boxed. He took lessons from 1904 under Professor Yamashita.

But it was not a one way street. Catch wrestling was introduced to Japan, and this is one of the routes from which MMA would emerge decades later.

American world heavyweight wrestling champion Lou Thesz became among the first to introduce Catch wrestling to Japan. Although Thesz's matches were largely, if not all, pre-determined, he was what the carnival wrestlers referred to as a 'hooker', meaning he could hook a submission hold on any opponent if he needed to.

He often 'competed' (in predetermined bouts, as per pro wrestling) against a Japanese former Shotokan practitioner named Rikidozan. The Japanese became a national hero in 'puroresu' (Japanese wrestling) for taking the American to the limit. Among Rikidozan's proteges was Antonio Inoki, the Japanese wrestling legend who would fight Muhammad Ali in another early MMA style bout.

Among the most successful Catch wrestlers in Europe were Billy Robinson and Karl Gotch. Robinson and Gotch trained in the original 'Snake Pit' in Wigan, where Catch wrestling was pioneered and from where coach Billy Riley taught hooks and chokes not taught in Greco Roman styles.

The National Wrestling Alliance (NWA) world heavyweight wrestling championship traces its lineage from George Hackenschmidt to Frank Gotch in 1905 through the likes of Lou Thesz. In 1981, Ric Flair, a Minnesota amateur wrestling champion who had been taught by wrestling champion and promotor Verne Gagne and Snake Pit legend Billy Robinson, became NWA champion for the first time. In 1991 Flair was stripped of his championship, leading to several new title claimants and the following year two of Lou Thesz's former trainees in Japan laid claim to the world wrestling championship. They were NWA champion Masahiro Chono and Union of Wrestling Forces International (UWFI) champion Nobuhiko Takada. Why the pro wrestling history lesson? It is because this marked a move away from American style puroresu in Japan and the beginning of what would become MMA.

In a ceremony with Thesz and Robinson, Takada was presented with Thesz's antique championship belt and proclaimed undisputed wrestling and martial arts champion. Takada beat boxer Trevor Berbick (who had defeated an old Muhammad Ali in his last fight) and proclaimed wrestling the strongest art in the world. Thesz, Robinson, Gotch and Takada opened a dojo in Tokyo called the Snakepit, after the original Wigan catch club where there were numerous style v style contests. Takada and his protégé Kazushi Sakuraba later feuded with UFC pioneers the Gracies and Takada went on to found the Pride MMA promotion.

Brazilian Jujutsu (BJJ) was also developing. Although Maeda was an exponent of Kodokan Judo BJJ would differentiate itself by a greater focus on grappling and ground work. The Gracie Family is synonymous with BJJ. The Gracie family would run 'Vale Tudo' ('anything goes') events where they would hone their BJJ skills. These Vale Tudo events would become the precursor of mixed martial arts tournaments.

Takada and his stable began a feud with the Brazilian Gracie family which saw Takada tapped out by Rickson Gracie, and only avenged when Kazushi Sakuraba defeated several of the Gracie brothers. Ironically Jujutsu was being represented by Westerners and Catch wrestling by Japanese! Canadian Karate and Jujutsu instructor Patrick McCarthy (9th dan Hanshi) was an early UWFI competitor and trained with Takada. McCarthy told me: *'Those years were wonderfully educational and I literally met and trained with the who's who of Japan's Kakutogi community. Our submission wrestling mentors were Karl Gotch, Billy Robinson, Lou Thesz and Danny Hodge, etc.'* Takada's 'shoot' wrestling organisation was the UWFI and similar outfits included Akira Maeda's RINGS and Minoru Suzuki's Pancrase.

In the 1970s Rorion Gracie, BJJ master and eldest son of Hélio Gracie, emigrated to the US, teaching BJJ. Rorion Gracie co-founded the Ultimate Fighting Championship (UFC). At the first UFC in 1993 Royce Gracie represented Jujutsu and Ken Shamrock represented shoot fighting. In 1993, Jujutsu and wrestling regained its legitimacy as Gracie and Shamrock battered boxers, Karateka and kickboxers. From the fusion of BJJ and shoot wrestling, the sport we now know as MMA emerged.

Among the British pioneers of MMA were Ian Freeman and Wigan's Tom Blackledge. Freeman had a boxing background but did train briefly in Jujutsu before getting experience in a Vale Tudo event. In early 2000, the UFC approached Ian Freeman to fight at UFC 24, where he lost to Scott Adams. He fought two more times in the UFC, winning both times. Later, Freeman's career hit a low point with four losses in a row, but he returned with a submission win in a rematch with Stanislav Nuschik. His greatest triumph was arguably his win on home soil over Frank Mir at UFC38.

Tom Blackledge trained in traditional Jujutsu (training alongside myself under Jaimie Lee-Barron), achieving 2nd dan before he went to the Wolfslair MMA gym in Widnes. Blackledge made his MMA debut in 2001 and fought at UFC 127 in 2011, later becoming a UFC coach.

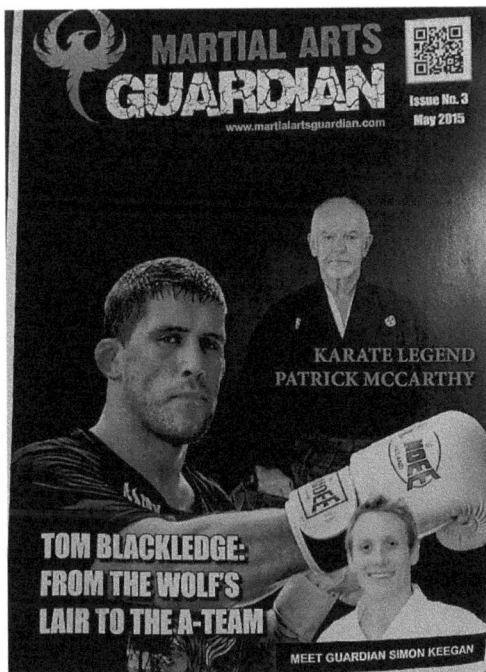

*Tom Blackledge, Patrick McCarthy and Simon Keegan
on the cover of Martial Arts Guardian magazine.*

Another early British pioneer into MMA was Andy Walker.

Andy Walker started learning Jujutsu in 1986 with Peter Clarke at the Leeds Kodokan Martial Arts Club, grading to 1st dan. Andy moved to Poole, Dorset in the mid 1990s, and despite his best efforts couldn't find a Jujutsu club so started his own. Andy then set about finding an association he could affiliate his club to, and organised meetings with Jimmy Pape (Bushido Ju Jitsu Academy, BJJA(GB)) and Allan Tattersall (UKJJAI).

The meeting with Allan Tattersall didn't materialise. Andy recalled: *'I met with Jimmy Pape in Liverpool and liked what he had to say and he invited me to join Bushido.'* In 1997 Poole Bushido Jujitsu Club was born. Not long after this Andy met up with training partner Rod Phelps (then 2nd dan Jujutsu) and struck up a friendship that would see them cross training with other martial arts including Judo and BJJ and start taking part in Vale Tudo events. Andy and Rod enjoyed success and started to get invited to shows. Both Andy and Rod were invited to fight on the bill of the first Cage Warriors show on 27th July, 2002, at York Hall in London. Subsequent stars of MMA and the UFC would make their name in Cage Warriors including Dan Hardy, Michael Bisping, and Conor McGregor. When Andy Walker started training for MMA it was truly mixed martial arts in that the competitors would come from different disciplines. However, as the sport gained in popularity MMA would develop as a style in its own right, in which practitioners no longer need to have a formal martial arts training in a particular discipline. In 2007, to try and improve and help the young fighters in the UK trying MMA Andy Walker started the MMA League. In a report advertising the MMA League Andy Walker discussed his thinking behind it: *'When I was younger every other weekend I was at some form of competition or other gaining valuable experience, but now with the frequent pro MMA shows around the country novice students are not gaining enough competition experience and I believe that not only the competitor is missing out but the British MMA scene also. With the popularity of MMA it made perfect sense to start a league which offers regular competitions for the novices, and even talented martial arts students who haven't made that transition to the pro scene.'* The MMA League would run for 6 years and amongst the young fighters Andy Walker helped was Gavin Davies.

Gavin Davies was born in 1984 and took up Jujutsu when he was 5 years old. Gavin said: *'My dad went to the local leisure centre to look at the martial arts on show and which one he would find suitable for me. He watched Aikido, Karate, Judo, and Jujutsu. At this time Paul Geoghegan was instructing the Jujutsu class and decided that was the art for his son.'* Certainly anyone having seen Paul Geoghegan on the mat can understand how one could be persuaded.

Picture of Gavin Davies (left) and Andy Walker (right).
[Picture provided by Gavin Davies of the Bushido Ju Jitsu Academy, BJJA(GB)]

The class in Wrexham would subsequently be taken on by one of Paul Geoghegan's students, Andy Pryce, who took Gavin to 1st dan in 1996 and 2nd dan in 2007. Inspired by the early UFC contests featuring Royce Gracie, Gavin started to cross train in other styles and took part in Andy Walker's MMA League. Soon Gavin was learning BJJ from Mick Broster in Walsall and from 2009 to 2012 was training MMA full time as part of Team Elite in Oswestry. Mick Broster would become the first person in the UK to receive a black belt from Eddie Bravo's 10th Planet Jiu-Jitsu. Davies was now enjoying considerable success in MMA and grappling tournaments, winning, amongst other titles, two elite NAGA titles: one in 2014 (Paris) and one in 2016 (London).

Training with the BJJA(GB) and the British Armed Forces. Present are the Navy, Army, and Royal Marines. Jimmy Pape and Martin Dixon with the instructors.
[Picture provided by Martin Dixon of the BJJA(GB)]

Martin Dixon at the BJJA(GB) National Championships
[Picture provided by Martin Dixon]

The boom in the popularity of BJJ had seen its spread around the world. One of the first pioneers to bring BJJ to the UK was Mauricio Gomes, one of only six men to be promoted to black belt (in 1981) by Rolls Gracie before his untimely death in a hang-gliding accident. Gomes married the daughter of Carlos Gracie (Reila). In the late 1990s Gomes arrived in the UK and started teaching BJJ through the Gracie Barra UK gyms. Gomes is also the father of BJJ champion Roger Gracie, who he helped bring to the UK and establish the Roger Gracie Academy, where he now helps teach. A notable student of the Roger Gracie Academy is 2nd dan Kevin Capel.

In 2015 the British Armed Forces added BJJ as an official combat training discipline. 2015 was also the year Gavin Davies joined the RAF. As the forces had officially adopted Jujutsu as a sport there was considerable support for those interested and capable of participating. This was perfect for Gavin, who joined the RAF Jujutsu club, which is called Legado BJJ and is instructed by Kevin Capel. Legado BJJ is also affiliated to the Roger Gracie Academy.

In addition to RAF and inter-service championships the forces teams compete in tournaments all over the world, where taking part is seen as a 'duty'. Gavin has continued to enjoy success and as a result of winning the International BJJ Federation (IBJJF) Pan-Pacific and Asian Open tournaments in 2016 (Melbourne) and 2017 (Tokyo) respectively he was awarded RAF Sports Personality of the Year 2017.

When asked who had been his inspiration Gavin stated: *'Royce and Helio Gracie; as I was always competing against bigger opponents [Gavin competes in the under 64 kg category] I loved watching Royce beat bigger opponents in the early UFC contests, and I loved reading stories about how Helio developed BJJ as he couldn't throw bigger opponents. Once you are on the ground, size goes out the window if you have technique.'*

It is a story that resonates throughout the history of Jujutsu. In the same way that Yukio Tani wowed audiences by beating much bigger opponents, superior skill continues to inspire.

In 2018 the British Armed Forces Ju Jitsu Association joined the BJJA(GB). BJJA(GB) coaches Martin Dixon and Jimmy Pape attended a coaching course with the Armed Forces where Roger Gracie was delivering a course. In keeping with Martin Dixon's broad church approach BJJ was welcomed into the BJJA(GB), and the British Armed Forces Jujutsuka are also now eligible for the BJJA(GB) competition format.

Epilogue

Today in the UK there are many strands of Jujutsu, far too many to cover comprehensively here.

The history of Jujutsu in the UK pre-WWII presented here is about as complete as possible. After the war, following the establishment of large organisations, governing bodies, and the massive increase in popularity of Jujutsu there were many splits, splinters, and new organisations formed. So much so that it would be completely impractical to cover them all in a book like this.

The omission of styles and teachers, many no doubt important and influential, is not a reflection on how I view their importance and nor does it diminish their contribution. I do think however that all Jujutsu strands in the UK should be able to trace their lineage back through the strands covered here where I identify some of the major early movements and influences.

In many respects the recent associations I discuss are representative examples of many such organisations practising Jujutsu in the UK.

Of course the proliferation of Jujutsu styles is not a recent phenomenon and in Edo Japan there were many hundreds of Jujutsu Ryu. As we have seen, there have been many important influences on the development of British Jujutsu. Perhaps we have revealed the most important with this book. Sadakazu Uyenishi (Raku) established his dojo in 1903.

His book *'The Text Book of Ju Jutsu as Practised in Japan'* (1905) was widely read and a standard text of the time. Furthermore, Uyenishi's students were also prolific authors of Jujutsu and formed the British Jujitsu Society (BJJS). Whilst Tani and Koizumi migrated to Judo, the BJJS continued to practise Jujutsu as taught by Uyenishi. Those practising Jujutsu during this time such as Harry H Hunter, Alf Morgan, Jim Hipkiss, and subsequently Jack Britten and Gerald Skyner, would also have likely been influenced.

We also discuss the influence of Kawaishi and many others, and of course, the Jujutsu of Bartitsu can still be seen within British Jujutsu.

Of course many subsequent developments by James Blundell, Robert Clark, Kenshiro Abbe, Vernon Bell and many others shape British Jujutsu as we know it today. When Tani and Uyenishi arrived in the UK the Jujutsu they taught was adapted to deal with British fighting styles such as wrestling and boxing, rapidly establishing a British Jujutsu style, which is unique from the Koryu parent styles. Indeed Chinese fighting styles were adapted to Japanese fighting methods in the establishment of some early Japanese Jujutsu Ryu. We see in British Jujutsu an evolution to a counter attacking form to boxing punches which is in contrast to the Koryu principle of Kobo ichi (attack and defence are one) described by Paul Masters.

In the latter part of the twentieth century some brought Koryu into the UK and continue to study this preferring the link to Japanese culture and practise. Many British Jujutsuka further developed styles by mixing martial arts, and of course there is now MMA.

However, what is clear is that Jujutsu has been critical in the development of martial arts in the UK and that British Jujutsu is very much alive.

It is important to note that the development of British Jujutsu suffered the intervention of two world wars. WWI (1914-1918) resulted in the deaths of over 1 million British men. WWII resulted in the deaths of over 400,000 Britons with almost as many wounded. The consequences of this for British Jujutsu are obvious and after each war British Jujutsu essentially had to reinvent itself. The difficulty in finding information and the absence of records limited the extent to which practiioners of British Jujutsu could define the lineage of their style, and thus the history became confused for many. Brazilian Jiu Jitsu in contrast has a clear lineage.

Sadakuza (Raku) Uyenishi was in the UK for only 7 years, yet we find his legacy is significant within British Jujutsu today.

It was Barton-Wright who took Uyenishi to London in 1900, but from the available evidence it would seem that it was the Jujutsu of Uyenishi that provided the greatest influence on the development of British Jujutsu. Thus I conclude with the thought, that although there have been many great pioneers of British Jujutsu, it is perhaps Uyenishi who should be considered as the person who laid the foundation for British Jujutsu as a style which is why the cover of this book is a tribute to his teachings.

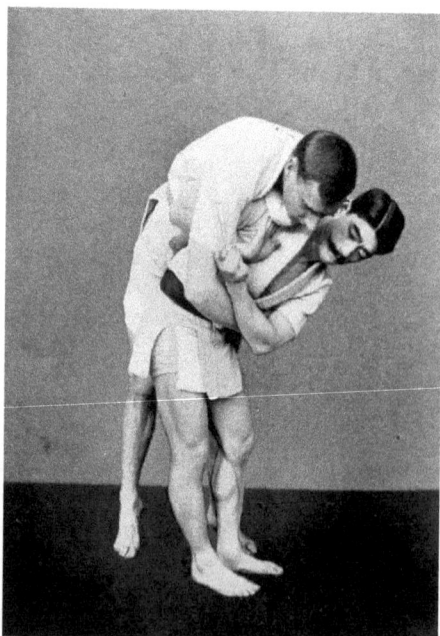

Raku Uyenishi: The father of British Jujutsu

Recommended Further Reading

Mol, S (2001). Classical Fighting Arts of Japan. **A Complete Guide to Koryu Jujutsu.**

Bowen, R (2011). **100 Years of Judo in Great Britain: Volume 1 Reclaiming of Its True Spirit.**

Bowen, R (2011). **100 Years of Judo in Great Britain: Volume 2 Reclaiming of Its True Spirit.**

Keegan, S (2018). **Karate Jutsu**

Layton, Clive (2002). **Shotokan Dawn: A selected early history of Shotokan Karate in Great Britain**

Tanaka, Fumon (2003). **Samurai Fighting Arts: The Spirit and the Practice**

DeMarco, Michael (2018). **Jujutsu & Judo in the West: Uke becomes Tori**

Hisatomi, T (1888). **Police Officer's Essential Illustrated Guide to Kempo**

Kano, Jigoro (1986). **Kodokan Judo**

Finn, Michael (1982). **Iaido the Way of the Sword**

Milton Giles (2002). **Samurai William**

Tani, Yukio (1958). **The Art of Ju-Jitsu**

Kawaishi, Mikonosuke (1957). **The Complete 7 Katas of Judo**

Kawaishi, Mikonosuke (1955). **My Method of Judo**

Uyenishi, Sadakazu (1905). **The text book of Ju-Jutsu as practised in Japan**

Sato, Shizuya **Nihon Jujutsu**

About the author

Simon Keegan is an instructor, researcher and author. He holds the grade of 6th dan and the traditional teaching title of Kyoshi. Keegan has trained under some of the senior Japanese and Chinese teachers in the world with his grades recognised by authority of the Japanese royal family and Shogun dynasty.

Simon Keegan was born to a martial arts family and studied from an early age. His father, David Keegan (5th dan), commenced Jujutsu study 60 years ago and is now a senior practitioner of both Japanese and Chinese martial arts, having lived and worked in the Far East. Before that, Simon's great uncle Bill Nelson trained to black belt in Jujutsu in two of the country's earliest Jujutsu clubs.

As a teenager Simon also became the 6th consecutive generation of his family to serve in the military. At the age of 16 Keegan was competing at national level in Karate, Kickboxing and Kobudo/Iaido while studying 'Bushidokan', a style derived from Shotokan, Budokan and Shukokai. In addition to Karate, the Bushido system taught by Steve Bullough also included Jujutsu, Aikido and Kenjutsu. He became his teacher's Uchideshi (senior indoor student and assistant instructor).

At the age of 22, Keegan moved over to Shobukan, a blend of Japanese Jujutsu, Shotokan Karate and the more Chinese/Malysian influenced Budokan Karate. Keegan first trained under Robert Carruthers and then his teacher Phil Handyside, a student of Budokan grandmaster Chew. Keegan was also studying traditional Jujutsu and graded 2nd dan in the Bugei Ju Hapan (18 martial arts including Jujutsu) at a grading in London.

On meeting the legendary Mitsuhiro Kondo Hanshi, one of the masters who introduced Karate and Aikido to Europe, Keegan joined Japan's oldest Budo fraternity, the Kokusai Budoin, of which he became a regional officer with his grades recognised by the hereditary shogun Tokugawa Yasuhisa. Keegan was invited to the unveiling of Tokugawa Ieyasu's treasures.

Keegan's Chinese martial arts studies over more than 20 years include Yang shi Taiji (Yang style Tai Chi), Sun shi (Sun Lu Tang's style) and Chinese sword. Keegan competed at European Wushu events, performed sword and Yang style in front of the mayor of Shanghai.

He also was awarded 2nd dan in Hirokazu Kanazawa's Shotokan division and Nihon Jujutsu under the late Shizuya Sato, later attaining 3rd dan in Nihon Jujutsu.

Keegan began studying Okinawan Goju Ryu Karate and Kobudo and was graded up to 3rd dan by Kyoshi Reiner Parsons, also training with headteacher and Kokusai Budoin chief director Tadanori Nobetsu 10th dan.

His father, David Keegan, was also a Kokusai Budoin member, predominantly training in the Iaido division under such Muso Jikiden Eishin Ryu masters as Keiji Tose, Yoshida and Iwasa.

Simon also began to pursue the old Karate Jutsu and Yawara methods. One of his teachers for 12 years was Hanshi Terry Wingrove, who studied Yawara under Yagyu Shingan Ryu master Sato Kimbei.

Keegan was made a regional director of Kokusai Budoin (IMAF) and International Director of IMAF GB, which later became the United Kingdom Budo Federation (UKBF) of which he is still a director. In 2006 he hosted the UKBF's first masters' course.

From 2007 he also studied Jujutsu with Hanshi Tattersall, who, as national director of Dai Nippon Butokukai, awarded UKBF the remit to award Shogo, and Keegan was awarded the title of Renshi.

Keegan also trained with students of the founder of Aikido, including the late Shihan Alan Ruddock. Keegan was later accepted into Dai Nippon Butokukai in the Jujutsu division (headed by Hamada Hanshi).

Keegan was awarded his 5th dan in Shobukan Karate by the headteacher in 2012, he graded in the same Dojo where Grandmaster Chew had taught Budokan to the club a generation earlier. He was later awarded 5th dan in Jujutsu and was awarded his 6th dan in Shobukan Karate in 2018.

Keegan has demonstrated his arts in Japanese cultural festivals and performed kata with the London Symphony Orchestra, the first person to ever do so. He has also trained with Kobudo, Batto Jutsu and Karate grandmaster Fumio Demura, who kindly wrote a foreword for Keegan's third book *Karate Jutsu*. Copies of it were acclaimed all over the world including in Japan and Okinawa.

In 2018 he competed in a charity boxing event which raised £140,000 for three charities, and met with the Honorary Consul of Japan and worked with the Japanese Embassy to make the UKBF part of the Japanese Season of Culture.

Keegan runs the Bushinkai Academy, headquartered in Manchester, and is technical director of the United Kingdom Budo Federation. As a senior student of Shihan Handyside he is one of a few tasked with carrying on the legacy of the Shobukan school for the next generation.

Glossary

Atemi waza – Body striking techniques.

Bashin - A double edge knife used to bleed horses.

Bojutsu – Martial art of using a bo staff.

Budo – Japanese martial arts. Literally 'way of preventing conflict.'

Budoka – Martial artist.

Bujutsu – Old term for 'martial techniques.'

Bushi – A Japanese term to describe warrior class.

Butoku Sai – Martial arts festival.

Daisho – 'Big and small': Japanese term for a matched pair of traditionally made Japanese swords worn by samurai.

Dan – Level. Synonymous with black belt grades, eg Shodan (black belt 1st dan).

Hakama are commonly worn in Aikijujutsu

Dojo – 'Place of the way': the training hall.

Edo (or Tokugawa) period – The era of Japanese history marked by Tokugawa Ieyasu becoming Shogun in 1603 up until the Meiji Restoration in 1868.

Gaijin - 'Outside person'. A Japanese term meaning a foreigner. A non-Japanese person, but usually referring to Westerners rather than, say, Chinese.

Gendai – Modern. In the context of martial arts, referring to schools developed after the Meiji Resoration.

Gi – A slang abbreviation/contraction of Kimono. The Kimono worn in Judo is called a Judogimono or Judogi for short, further contracted to 'gi.' Generally in modern times refers to both the jacket and trousers.

The white Gi is typical of Jujutsu, Judo and Karate

Hakama – Formal clothing worn over the kimono. They are baggy trousers rather like culottes with seven pleats. They were originally for horse-riding. In martial arts they are most commonly associated with Aikido, Kendo, Iaido, Kyudo and Koryu Bujutsu. They are very seldom worn for Karate or Judo.

Hakuda – 'White strike': a term, also written 'baida', used in southwestern Japan to refer to a mostly percussive method of Jujutsu derived from Chinese Quanfa (Kempo). Famous practitioners include Akiyama Yoshitoki of Yoshin Ryu.

Iaido is commonly taught as part of Jujutsu

Hananejibo – A baton used to control horses. Adopted as a makeshift weapon in Yagyu Shingan Ryu.

Hanshi – Model teacher. A Shogo (teaching title) issued by organisations like the Dai Nippon Butoku Kai and Kokusai Budoin. It is typically issued after the grade of 8th dan.

Hiden Mokuroku – 'Initiated into the secrets', a menkyo (teaching scroll) issued by styles such as Daito Ryu. This was the certificate Minoru Mochizuki held in Daito Ryu. The Mokuroku may refer to a 'catalogue' of techniques and 'hiden' means secrets. A clumsy analogy may be to compare it roughly to 2nd or 3rd dan.

Hojo - Hojo Jutsu is the art of tying and restraining with a rope or cord.

Iaido – The Japanese art of drawing the sword from its scabbard, cutting an opponent, removing blood from the blade, and replacing the sword.

Iemoto – A term used to refer to the founder, or the current Grand Master of school, used synonymously with the word Soke.

Jingama – A type of kama (hand held sickle) used in styles such as Yagyu Shingan Ryu.

Jodo – Japanese martial art using the short staff, or Jo.

Judoka – A person who practises Judo.

Jujutsuka – A person who practises Jujutsu.

Jutte – A kind of truncheon similar to the Okinawan Sai (pictured below).

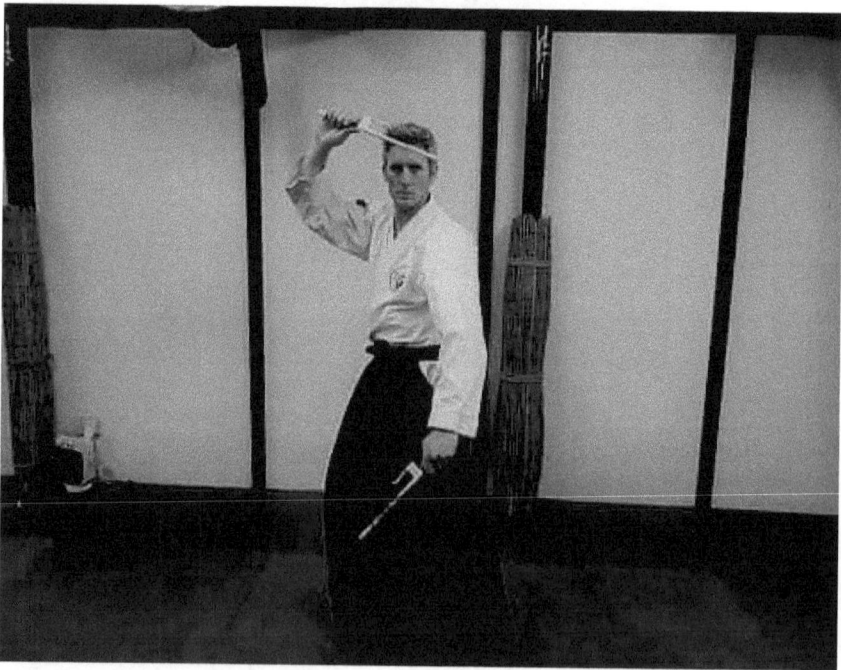

Kata – A choreographed pattern of movements practised alone or with a partner.

Katana – Traditional Japanese sword used by samurai.

Kenjutsu – Umbrella term for Koryu schools of Japanese swordsmanship.

Kobudo – Literally, old martial ways; typically refers to Okinawan weapons (Nunchaku, Sai, Tonfa etc) but can also, and to a lesser extent, refer to Japanese Koryu Bujutsu.

Koryu – Martial arts schools in Japan established before the Meiji Restoration of 1868.

Koshi no Mawari – 'around the hips', a term used by styles such as Takenouchi Ryu. It refers to unarmed combat when the sword and shortsword are still sheathed in the belt.

Kusarigamajutsu – The Japanese art of using the weapon kusarigama (a sickle on a chain). See below:

Kyoju Dairi – Representative head-teacher. A term used in styles such as Daito Ryu for one who is the de facto head-teacher of the style when the actual inheritor is still alive but may be retired. Yoshida Kotaro held this title.

Kyoshi – Exemplary teacher or Professor. A Shogo awarded by organisations such as Dai Nippon Butoku Kai and Kokusai Budoin, usually at around

6th or 7th dan.

Kyu – Denotes a level below black belt or dan grade.

Makimono – Scrolls of proficiency. See below:

Menkyo Kaiden – Licence of total transmission. The holder is able to teach the entire curriculum.

Menkyo Mokuroku – See Hiden Mokuroku.

Menkyo Oku Iri – In koryu (old styles) that issued menkyo (scroll of competency), Okuiri (entrance to the secrets) was often the first scroll awarded. It may be considered similar to the modern grade of 1st dan.

Nabebutajutsu – Fighting with a makeshift shield (such as a saucepan lid). This art was studied by early Bartitsu practitioners.

Naginatajutsu - The Japanese martial art of using the naginata. See below:

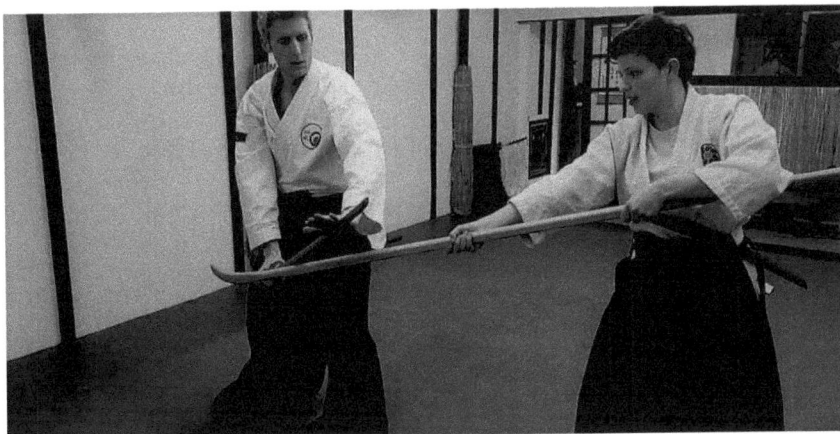

Newaza – Grappling or fighting on the ground.

Nidan – A 2nd dan black belt.

Nitojutsu – Fighting with two long swords. Miyamoto Musashi was a notable exponent of this.

Randori – Refers to free practice, usually in Judo where it is one versus one.

Renshi – A Shogo meaning 'polished teacher'. It is typically awarded at around 4th or 5th dan.

Ryu – School or flow. For example Kito Ryu, Daito Ryu. A homonym of Ryu would also be dragon.

Ryuha – A school passed on by hereditary transmission.

Saikoo Komon – Awarded as the title of most valuable technical advisor.

Samurai – Military nobility and officer caste of medieval and early-modern Japan.

Sengoku period – Approx. 1467 to approx. 1600, in Japan marked by near-constant military conflict. The Sengoku period came to an end when the Tokugawa shogunate was established (Edo period).

Sensei – Martial arts teacher. Literally 'one who has gone before.'

Shihan – A senior or master instructor of martial arts.

Shodan – A 1st dan black belt.

Shogo – A teaching title awarded by organisations such as the Dai Nippon Butoku Kai. They originated as advancements beyond 5th dan.

Shogun – The military dictator of Japan from 1185 to 1868.

Shurikenjutsu - Japanese martial arts of throwing shuriken.

Sojutsu - Japanese martial art of fighting with a Japanese spear.

Soke – Head master, or grand master of a school or ryu.

Sosai – Japanese word for 'President'.

Tachi – A type of traditional Japanese sword worn by samurai.

Taijutsu – Body art. Another term for Jujutsu that is often synonymous with the unarmed combat methods of Ninjutsu.

Tassha – The first scroll awarded in Takenouchi Ryu. Possibly derived from 'one who has Tatsu' (mastered). Tatsujin (master), Tasseru (to become expert in), Tassei (to achieve).

Tessen – A Japanese war fan. See below:

Tori - The executor of a technique in partnered martial arts practice.

Torite – 'Receiving hand' a term used in styles like Takenouchi Ryu and

Yagyu Shingan Ryu and referring to escapes through manipulation. Similar to the Chinese concept of Chin na.

Uke - The person who receives the technique in partnered martial arts practice.

Wakizashi – A short sword worn by samurai. Also known as Kodachi. See below:

By the Same Author:
Karate Jutsu: History and Evolution of the Okinawan Martial Art

The origins of Karate are shrouded in mythology and a book that tells the art's complete history is both necessary and timely. The art of Karate was developed in the Ryukyu Kingdom, now Okinawa, over hundreds of years. Like many martial arts it was once designed to main, disable or kill but has since become adapted into a way of life and a sport that is seen in both the UFC and in 2020 makes its Olympic debut.

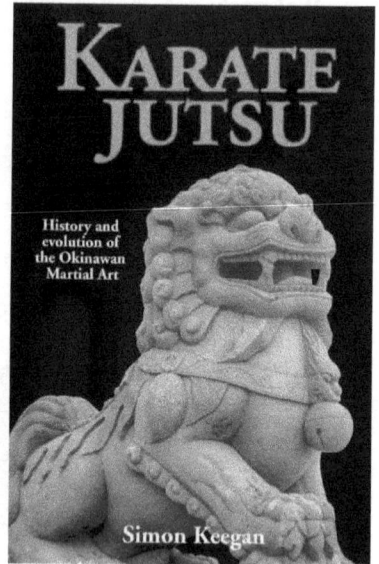

It's a must for any Karateka to read time and time again to understand the origins of Karate and its structure, and essential for the bookshelf of any serious martial artist – *Steve Rowe 9th Dan*

Simon Keegan has a true passion when it comes to the martial arts. It is a special breed of man who lives the arts, rather than just doing them. He is without a doubt one of the true guardians of the history of the arts. They are in good hands – *Alfie Lewis 9th Dan*

I was immediately impressed with the quality of Keegan's articles. So I knew his book would be a well-researched, well-documented, and enlightening text. It ties down many of the loose ends and nagging questions that have existed for many years – *Jim Mather 9th Dan*

Simon is skilled in the history of quite a number of martial arts of Japan, China and other eastern arts. I would recommend that you read this and his other works – *Phil Handyside 9th Dan*

I am glad to be part of Simon's effort to share knowledge of the history of Karate with this book – *Fumio Demura 9th Dan*

Simon has earned his place as a modern day Sherlock Holmes determining the true origins of Karate and separating the fact from the fiction which abounds martial arts – *Terry Wingrove 9th Dan*

172

Index of key Jujutsu practitioners referenced in this book

Lightning Source UK Ltd.
Milton Keynes UK
UKHW021816020220
358027UK00014B/289